Are you ready to have some fun?

Thank you so much for ordering the Pre-K YOUR Way Curriculum Series. I created these activities to support caring parents and teachers like you in creating meaningful learning experience for your children. I hope you enjoy these activities as much as I enjoyed creating them.

Please contact me with any questions or comments that you have while working through the curriculum booklet. I want to hear from **YOU!**

If you enjoy these activities, please write a review on the product that you purchased. All products can be found at:

www.jdeducational.com

Happy Playing, Learning and Growing!

Sincerely,

Jeana Kinne

ISBN-13: 978-1723586361

DEDICATION

This Curriculum Series is dedicated to all parents and teachers striving to provide optimal learning opportunities for the children in their care. Thank you for your patience, love and support in nurturing little minds, creating a positive impact on our future generations.

DISCLAIMER

JDEducational and the author is not to be held responsible for injury or damage created or caused while preparing for or completing the activities in this book. Adult supervision, safety and caution should be used at all times. Do not leave children unattended while completing these activities.

Pre-K Your Way Activity Series

© 2018 JDEducational
Curriculum Series materials may not be copied or distributed without written permission of
JD Educational. Additional curriculum can be purchased at www.jdeducational.com

About Our Curriculum

Our Curriculum is designed to strengthen school readiness by meeting the identified skills and concepts, which are necessary for a smooth transition to Kindergarten. These curriculum modules include low-cost/no-cost activities which parents, preschool staff and home daycare providers can use with the children in their care.

This curriculum was developed using current Kindergarten Readiness Assessments including: Common Core Kindergarten Standards, the Preschool Learning Foundation and the Desired Results Developmental Profile.

This curriculum addresses the following areas of development:

- Cognitive Development
- Mathematical Development
- Physical Development
- Language Development
- Literacy Development
- Social-Emotional Development
- Self-Help Skill Development

This curriculum was developed to meet the interests of all children and based on the multiple intelligences theory by Howard Gardner. Gardner was a Harvard University Professor who believed that traditional education wasn't utilizing the strengths of all children. Every child is unique and learns differently. Gardner identified eight different "intelligences" and pathways to learning.

These eight intelligences include:

1. Linguistic – "word smart"
2. Logical-Mathematical –"numbers/reasoning smart"
3. Spatial - "picture smart"
4. Bodily-Kinesthetic – "movement smart"
5. Musical – "Rhythms and songs smart"
6. Interpersonal – "People smart"
7. Intrapersonal – "Self smart"
8. Naturalist – "outdoors/nature smart"

Learning Objectives - Level 3

After completing all modules in the Level 2 Curriculum Series, the child should be able to:

Mathematics
- Solve simple addition and subtractions problems with objects.
- Count up to 20 objects, using one to one correspondence.
- Recognizes the names of Numerals.
- Understands size words (Smaller vs. Larger).
- Describe shapes by at least two characteristics.
- Complete patterns that have two or more elements.
- Sort objects into groups by two or more attributes.
- Show understanding of measurement by using measuring tools.

Science
- Demonstrate Curiosity and ask Questions
- Engage in problem solving techniques.
- Use words to discuss predictions
- Use language to reiterate process and conclusions
- Use a variety of techniques to record information and data collection
- Use language to describe objects by a variety of attributes
- Demonstrate understanding of differences between people, animals, plants and other parts of the planet.
- Complete multi-step projects.

Language and Literacy
- Write their own name, without help.
- Follow three-step directions.
- Use sentences in conversation to describe, explain or predict outcomes of real or imaginary events.
- Initiate and engage in literacy activities.
- Write familiar words by looking at the word then copying.
- Identify all letters by sight and sound

Problem Solving Skills
- Predict the results of a familiar action.
- Develop strategies to solve a problem.
- Communicate memories about a sequence of related events that happened in the past.
- Put materials or objects together in new and inventive ways.
- Participate in challenging multi-step activities.

Gross Motor/Fine Motor Development
- Participate in a variety of gross motor activities that require balance and coordination.
- Hop on one foot five or more times.
- Use scissors to cut out an object.
- Use a pen or marker to write familiar words.

- Use a pencil to trace new words.

JDEducational
Play · Learn · Grow

Contents at a Glance

Module1: Camping Adventures

- Part1: Camping Themed Learning Activities
- Part 2: Camping Project

Module 2: Transportation Activities

- Part 1: Transportation Themed Learning Activities
- Part 2: Transportation Projects

Module 3: Discovering Weather Activities

- Part 1: Weather Themed Learning Activities
- Part 2: Weather Projects

Module 4: Planet Earth

- Part 1: Planet Earth Themed Activities
- Part 2: Plane Earth Projects

Module 5: Construction: Building Components and Design Activities

- Part 1: Construction Themed Learning Activities
- Part 2: Construction Projects

Module 6: Oceanography - The Five Oceans and What Lives Within

- Part 1: Ocean Themed Learning Activities
- Part 2: Oceanography Projects

JDEducational
Play · Learn · Grow

Table of Contents
Each unit builds on concepts learned in the previous unit.
Activities within each unity may be completed in any order desired.

Setting up an Indoor Learning Environment at Home

Home-based learning environments tend to be one of the most complicated and multi-functional spaces in a home. Not only do parents need to make room for the variety of crafts, toys and other materials, there also needs to be space for adults. A home is not only for learning and growing, but also a place where spending time together as a family is key. So, as a parent, where do you put all of this stuff without it taking over the entire home? Creating a simple, organized and mess-free play space is a large task, but with some pre-planning, it is possible.

Finding that "right" space where there isn't a lot of foot traffic is extremely important. Spend two days observing the common areas of your home. While doing this, make some mental notes as to what areas aren't used often and where adults tend to gather. If there's a corner or a wall of a common room that isn't needed on a regular basis, that's the perfect spot for a play area. When a child is playing, she/he is tapping into their creativity and telling a story. Waiting until the child finishes their play allows that child to complete their story they were creating, whether it's with a baby doll, building blocks, cars and trains - or another favorite toy. Completing tasks without constant interruptions will allow a child to form a beginning, middle and end (a full-circle) of play.

Next, what you should place in this learning environment is dependent on the child's age and developmental level. A toddler will play with something different then a five year old. No matter what age the child is, there are certain "must haves" for their space. These include: a quiet spot (either a bean bag or large pillow), books, puzzles, stuffed animals or baby dolls, an assortment of blocks, art materials and plastic or wood animals. When there are multiple-aged children in your home, be sure to give each one their own space, either by separating their areas - or using two different types of shelving units to visually demonstrate what is theirs.

Organizing materials into functional and workable environments will support the process of learning in a practical, step-by-step fashion. This ensures that the space is easily kept clean and visually pleasing. Each toy should have it's own dedicated space. For small objects, sort them by category and place them in small baskets or plastic bins (balls, cars and trucks, train tracks, books, paper, crayons, etc). If possible, take a picture of the items when they're separated and attach the pictures to their appropriate bin or basket. These containers can be placed on the floor or in a shelving unit against the wall. Provide a children's table, or allow them to take artwork to the main table in your home.

Sometimes children have too many different toys, which can cause toy chaos. Pick out no more than ten to twelve toys, which fall into the categories listed in the above paragraph. Place the rest of the items into large plastic storage bins and put them in a closet, garage or outdoor shed. Children will get bored when they play with the same toys over and over again. A typical toy rotation schedule is every three to four weeks, although some children get tired of toys quicker than others. If you notice the child becomes less engaged with the materials that are set out, rotate them with some of the materials that you put into storage bins. Watch as the child rediscovers their love for a toy they had previously lost interest in.

Lastly, learning to put away toys and stay organized at an early age helps prevent clutter over time - and will also teach children respect for their items. To make sure that the child takes ownership and pride in keeping the play area clean from the start, insist that they every time they are finished with a project or an activity in their play area, they clean up before they transition to another part of the home. Remember to always praise them with "Thank you for listening" or "Wow, you did that all by yourself" when they finish.

If clean up time is a struggle, encourage them to clean up by trying these ideas:

- **Play a clean-up game:** Using your watch, have a race against the clock! How long will it take them to put the toys away?

- **Sing a Song:** The Barney "Clean- Up" Song is a very popular choice.

- **Use this time as a Teachable Moment:** "Let's put all of the red things away first! Can you find all the red items?"

- **Help Out:** Having some help from a parent tends to be a motivator. Example: "You put the trucks away and I will put the balls away".

Pre-K YOUR Way

Level 3 Unit 1

Camping Adventures
Outdoor Exploration Project

Camping Themed Items For Indoor Learning Environment

Now that you have set up your environment, you are ready to place materials in it that directly relate to the theme you are studying! Here are some suggestions of materials your child can free-play with during the "Exploring My Community" Theme:

Books: Age-appropriate books that directly correlate with the monthly theme can be found at your local library or bought separately online. This is a great opportunity to take a trip with your child to your local library and go on a search together. Have them identify words or pictures on the cover of children's books that correlate to the theme. Place a variety of books related to the theme in your child's book area. This will increase opportunities for them to expand their knowledge and use what they learn in the activities to comprehend what they read in the books.

These are age-appropriate books that directly correlate with the monthly theme, which can be found at your local library or bought separately online.

1) Curious George Goes Camping – by Margret Rey and H.A. Re

2) Going Camping – by Cathy Beyton

3) Maisy Goes Camping – by Lucy Cousins

4) Fred and Ted Goes Camping – by Peter Eastman

5) Just Me and My Dad– by Mercer Mayer

6) S is for S'mores: A Camping Alphabet – by Helen Foster James

7) Goldilocks and the Three Bears – by Jan Brett

8) We're Going on a Bear Hunt – by Michael Rosen and Helen Oxenbury

Art Area: Encourage your child use this throughout each day by rotating items in an art area. These can be items have already been painted on, paper that they drew on already or leftover materials from another project. Thought provoking art projects are created when children are given unlimited opportunities to explore a variety of materials.

Some suggestions for the art area include:
- Crayons
- Paper
- Pens
- Empty Boxes (all kinds)
- Empty Toilet Paper or Paper Towel Rolls
- Foil
- Clean Q-tips for painting
- Scraps of paper
- Scraps of Yarn
- Scraps of any type of material – including fabric, sand paper, etc.
- Paper Bags
- Straws
- Popsicle Sticks
- Anything else that can be reused.

Suggested Cooking Activities

These are simple cooking and snack-time activities that correlate with the theme. The children can prepare these snacks with adult assistance.

1) **Trail Mix:**

   Place each of the following food items in their own bowl, with a separate spoon: popcorn, almonds, peanuts, chocolate chips, small marshmallows, raisons and pretzels. Tell the child to use the spoon to put **one** scoop of each ingredient into a zip-lock baggie! Have them shake it and mix it up.

2) **SMORES!**

   Allow the child to pick out two graham crackers. Encourage them to place one piece of chocolate and one marshmallow in between the graham crackers to make a sandwich. Next, the adult should microwave the snack on high until they melt together. Enjoy!

Sensory Bin Suggestions

A sensory bin is a small plastic bucket that is filled with a variety of materials. Sensory bins provide a space to engage in sensory-rich activities that offer opportunities to investigate textures while providing activities for relaxation and self-regulation. Sensory bins encourage language development, small motor development and control, spatial concepts, problem-solving skills and scientific observations. Each month there are suggested sensory bin materials that correlate with the theme of the unit.

Set Up Instructions: In a Plastic Bucket, rotate the following sensory activities throughout the month.

1) **Sand Writing Table:**

   Mix 2 cups of sand, 1 ½ cups cold water and 1 cup of cornstarch together. Stir the mixture for five to ten minutes over medium heat until it becomes thick. Pour the thick sand onto a cookie sheet. After it cools, have your child practice writing the Letter of the Week, Number of the Week and drawing the Shape of the Week in the sand.
   Note: You can also use this mixture to build sand castles that will stick together longer.

2) **On the Ground:**

   When a child goes camping, they discover so many natural items that are left on the ground. Fill up the sensory bucket with leaves, pinecones, weeds, flowers, sticks and river rocks. Encourage the child to touch each item and describe how each item feels. Do they crinkle when you hold them? If you have small plastic people or jungle animals, add them to the box to create pretend play options.

Dramatic Play Area

This play area allows children to understand and experience the adult world through imitation and creativity. The dramatic play area provides a safe space for young children to create stories while practicing new vocabulary and practicing social skills. It is also a space where groups of children engage in pretend play which provides opportunities to learn self-help skills, share space and materials, take turns and the use abstract thinking. Each month there is a list of suggested materials to integrate into this area, which correlate with the theme of the month.

Suggested props to include in the dramatic play/pretend play area include:

- Small Pop-up tent
- Sleeping Bag
- Blanket
- Duffel bag/suitcase
- Fishing Hat
- Sunglasses
- Backpack
- Binoculars
- Plastic fish
- Plastic cooking materials
- Empty bucket
- Small tree limbs/sticks for firewood
- Blow up raft or inner tube w/ Long sticks (for fishing)

Learning Objectives - Level 3

After completing all modules in the Level 3 Curriculum Series, the child should be able to:

Mathematics
- o Solve simple addition and subtractions problems with objects.
- o Count up to 20 objects, using one to one correspondence.
- o Recognizes the names of Numerals.
- o Understands size words (Smaller vs. Larger).
- o Describe shapes by at least two characteristics.
- o Complete patterns that have two or more elements.
- o Sort objects into groups by two or more attributes.
- o Show understanding of measurement by using measuring tools.

Science
- o Demonstrate Curiosity and ask Questions
- o Engage in problem solving techniques.
- o Use words to discuss predictions
- o Use language to reiterate process and conclusions
- o Use a variety of techniques to record information and data collection
- o Use language to describe objects by a variety of attributes
- o Demonstrate understanding of differences between people, animals, plants and other parts of the planet.
- o Complete multi-step projects.

Language and Literacy
- o Write their own name, without help.
- o Follow three-step directions.
- o Use sentences in conversation to describe, explain or predict outcomes of real or imaginary events.
- o Initiate and engage in literacy activities.
- o Write familiar words by looking at the word then copying.
- o Identify all letters by sight and sound

Problem Solving Skills
- o Predict the results of a familiar action.
- o Develop strategies to solve a problem.
- o Communicate memories about a sequence of related events that happened in the past.
- o Put materials or objects together in new and inventive ways.
- o Participate in challenging multi-step activities.

Gross Motor/Fine Motor Development
- o Participate in a variety of gross motor activities that require balance and coordination.
- o Hop on one foot five or more times.
- o Use scissors to cut out an object.
- o Use a pen or marker to write familiar words.
- o Use a pencil to trace new words

Part 1: Outdoor Exploration Academic Activities

These activities have been developed to meet specific, age-appropriate, Kindergarten-Readiness skills. These skills are specified in the learning objectives of each activity. The following activities may be completed in any order desired and are specifically designed to address the academic domains: math, science, language, literacy, cognitive, problem solving, and physical development.

Each activity is on its own page. If the adult chooses to print the activities, the space below each activity is provided for adults to write notes regarding the activity. Adults are encouraged to note if the child enjoyed the activity and if the child needs to work on specific learning objectives. Each activity can be repeated more than once to enable the child to master the learning objectives designed for that activity.

A. Math/Science Development

    1. Going on a Backpacking Trip
    2. Trail Maps and Directions
    3. Goldilocks and the Three Bears
    4. Tree Branch Count
    5. Campfire Crackle

B. Language/Literacy Development

    1. Tent Stories
    2. In the Dark, Dark Night
    3. Going on a Bear Hunt
    4. Camping Word Bank
    5. Stick Name

C. Physical Development- Gross Motor & Fine-Motor

    1. Tracing Nature
    2. Edible Tent
    3. Following the Leader – Obstacle Course
    4. Tree Tag - Leaf Collection
    5. Spider Web Jump

Mathematical Development – Understanding Numbers and their Purpose

By Completing Level 3 Activities, We will learn how to...

- o Solve simple addition and subtractions problems with objects.
- o Count up to 20 objects, using one to one correspondence.
- o Recognizes the names of Numerals.
- o Understands size words (Smaller vs. Larger).
- o Describe shapes by at least two characteristics.
- o Complete patterns that have two or more elements.
- o Sort objects into groups by two or more attributes.
- o Show understanding of measurement by using measuring tools.

Science/Cognitive Development – Learning How to Solve Problems

By Completing Level 3 Activities, We will learn how to..

- o Demonstrate Curiosity and ask Questions
- o Engage in problem solving techniques.
- o Use words to discuss predictions
- o Use language to reiterate process and conclusions
- o Use a variety of techniques to record information and data collection
- o Use language to describe objects by a variety of attributes
- o Demonstrate understanding of differences between people, animals, plants and other parts of the planet.
- o Complete multi-step projects.

A1. Our Exploration Trip - Activity time: 30 minutes

Materials Needed
- ☐ Two (2) Empty toilet paper rolls or One (1) Empty paper towel roll cut in half
- ☐ One (1) Roll of Scotch Tape
- ☐ One (1) Package of Markers
- ☐ One (1) Camera (or Smartphone camera)
- ☐ Outdoor Area – Beach, Park, River, Forest, etc.
- ☐ Access to a Computer and Printer

Instructions:

Step 1: Tell the child you are going on a Nature Hunt.

Step 2: In order to do this, we will need binoculars.

Step 3: The adult should tape the two empty toilet paper rolls together, side by side.

Step 4: Allow the child to decorate the binoculars with markers.

Step 5: Take a walk to an outdoor area of your choosing (see the materials list for examples).

Step 6: Tell the child to walk around, using their binoculars to find 10 interesting animals and objects.

Step 7: When the child finds something, take a picture of it with your camera.

Step 8: Once the child found 10 items, return home and print the pictures on blank paper.

Step 9: Staple all the pictures together to make a book.

Step 10: Ask them what each picture is and write down the name of the picture on the corresponding page.

Step 11: Leave the book in the child's book area so they can share it with others.

A.1 Learning Objectives

Math/Science	Language/Literacy	Problem Solving	Motor Skills
• One to One Correspondence • Counting 1-10	• Memory • Introduction to Creating Stories	• Cause and Effect • Curiosity and Initiative • Engagement and Persistence	• Fine Motor: Using a marker

Notes: What did your child do well? Are there any skills they need to continue to work on?

A2. Trail Maps and Directions - Activity time: 20 to 30 minutes

Materials Needed

☐ One (1) Printed Map of your neighborhood or one (1) printed map of a local child-friendly trail (Maps can be printed from Mapquest.com or Google maps for free)
☐ One (1) Pen
☐ One (1) way to access a video on the Internet.

Instructions:

Step 1: Watch the following YouTube video and act out the song with the child:

Move Left! Directions Songs for Kids
by Dream English Kids. **https://www.youtube.com/watch?v=Vgyer0lauyQ**

Step 2: It's time to go on a walk. Explain to the child that following directions are important in preventing people from getting lost.

Step 3: Use the map of your neighborhood to draw a line of where you're going to walk and what turns you're going to make.

Step 4: Using the map, go on a walk with the child. Follow the path outlined in Step 3. Each time you turn, have the child say if you are going right or left.

Step 5: At each turn, ask the child to use a pen to mark off where they are on the map.

Step 6: When you end up back at your house, show the map to the child so they can see where they went.

Take it to the next level:

Step 6: Print out a map from your home to a home of a friend or relative that lives close by (or other location).

Step 7: Draw the route you're going to take on the map.

Step 8: Give the map to the child before you get into the car and see if they can follow along throughout your drive.

Step 9: Show them where you are starting from and where you are ending. While in the car, ask you child what direction you are going (right, left, etc).

A.2 Learning Objectives

Math/Science	Language/Literacy	Problem Solving	Motor Skills
• Introduction to Measurements • Introduction to Maps	• Following Multiple-Step Directions • Building Vocabulary (Right vs. Left)	• Cause and Effect • Directions • Memory and Knowledge • Geographical Investigation	• Fine Motor: Using a Pen or Marker to Draw

Notes: What did your child do well? Are there any skills they need to continue to work on?

A3. Camping Opposites - Activity time: 20 minutes

Materials Needed
• The book "Goldilocks and the Three Bears" or access to the internet

Instructions:

Step 1: Read the book, "Goldilocks and the Three Bears", by Robert Southey. If you don't have the book, visit your local library or search the Internet for a video of the book being read. An example is here: https://www.youtube.com/watch?v=KndSVsY5HWM

Step 2: Tell the child you're going to talk about "opposites" in the story. Explain to the child what the word **"Opposite"** means: **How characteristics of objects differ from one another.** For example, if something is "hot", the opposite is "cold"

Step 3: Ask the child what the opposite of the following words are. These are the "opposites" that were in the story they just listened to. The adult should say the first word and see if the child can come up with the underlined word on their own.

- Big vs. _Small_
- Hard vs. _Soft_
- Asleep vs. Awake
- In vs. Out
- Hungry vs. Full

Step 4: Now let's talk about **opposites** that you would see outside while camping. Can the children think of items or animals that fit these opposite categories:

- Up vs. Down (Example: Bird vs. Ant)
- Long vs. Short (Example: Worm vs. Rock)
- Wet vs. Dry (Example: Ocean vs. Sand)
- Dirty vs. Clean (Example: Mud vs. Water)

Step 5: Can you or the child think of more opposites?

A.3 Learning Objectives

Math/Science	Language/Literacy	Problem Solving	Motor Skills
•N/A	•Using Language in Conversation •Memory	•Memory and Knowledge •Curiosity and Initative •Engagement and Persistence •Use language to reiterate process and conclusions •Use language to describe objects by a variety of attributes •Demonstrate understanding of differences between objects.	•Fine Motor: Using a Pen or Marker to Draw

Notes: What did your child do well? Are there any skills they need to continue to work on?

A4. Tree Branch Count - Activity time: 20 minutes

Materials Needed
- ☐ Four (4) Sheets of blank paper
- ☐ One (1) Box of crayons
- ☐ One (1) Black marker or pen
- ☐ Twenty (30) ¾ inch round stickers (Also known as color coding labels)

Instructions:

Step 1: Lay four pieces of blank paper on the table in front of the child.

Step 2: Tell the child there are a lot of different trees in the forest. Each tree is special and unique. All trees have a different number of branches and leaves.

Step 3: Tell the child they're going to draw four different trees. Each tree will have a different number of branches.

Step 4: Tell the child to draw one tree on the first piece of paper. This tree should **have eight branches.**

Step 5: Tell the child to draw one tree on the second piece of paper **that has six branches**.

Step 6: Tell the child to draw one tree on the third piece of paper **that has four branches.**

Step 7: Tell the child to draw one tree on the last piece of paper **that has two branches.**

Step 8: Next, tell the child to put one **round sticker on every tree branch they drew** in Steps 4 through 7.

Step 9: When completed, tell the child to number the stickers on the **first tree.** They should write the numbers one through eight, one number on each round sticker.

Step 10: Tell the child to write numbers one through six on the **second tree**, writing one number on each round sticker.

Step 11: Tell the child to write numbers one through four on the **third tree**, writing one number on each round sticker.

Step 12: Tell the child to write numbers one and two on the **fourth tree**, writing one number on each round sticker.

Step 13: Next, ask the child to count how many branches are on the first tree and then count how many branches are on the second tree. Ask your child to write the number on the piece of paper (write 8 on the tree that has 8 branches and write 6 on the tree that has 6 branches).

Step 14: Ask them which one has more branches? Which number is larger: 8 or 6?

Step 15: Ask the child the following question:
"How many more branches does the first tree have than the second tree?"

Step 16: To find out the answer to this question, we need to subtract! Ask them to put one round sticker on eight of their fingers.

Step 17: Ask your child to count six of the fingers that have stickers on them.

Step 18: Ask them how many more fingers have stickers on them? (Answer: 2)

Step 19: Ask them to repeat the following phrase:

"Eight **minus** Six Equals Two. The first tree has two **more** branches than the second tree. The second tree has two branches **less** than the first tree."

Step 20: Repeat Steps 13 through 19, asking the child to count the difference between the total number of branches on the following trees:

- Second tree and the third trees?
- The third tree and the fourth trees?
- The fourth tree and the first trees?

Step 21: Ask the child to count the total number of branches on all four trees:
(8 branches + 6 branches + 4 branches + 2 branches = 20 branches).

Step 22: Take a walk around your neighborhood and look at all the trees. Ask your child the following questions:

- How many branches are there in the trees?
- Are there some branches that are straight and others that are curvy?
- Are there some branches that are thick and others that are thin?
- Ask them to find the tree in their neighborhood that has the most branches on it.

A.4 Learning Objectives

Math/Science	Language/Literacy	Problem Solving	Motor Skills
• One to One Correspondence • Introduction to Addition Introduction to Subtraction • Number Identification • Writing Numbers	• Using new Vocabulary (More vs. Less)	• Memory and Knowledge • Curiosity and Initative • Engagement and Persistence • Use language to reiterate process and conclusions • Demonstrate understanding of differences between objects.	• Fine Motor: Using a Pen or Marker to Draw • Fine Motor: Peeling Stickers

Notes: What did your child do well? Are there any skills they need to continue to work on?

A5. Campfire Crackle - Activity time: 20 minutes

Materials Needed
- ☐ Ten (10) or more Sticks
- ☐ One (1) Blanket
- ☐ Four (4) Plastic Easter Eggs
- ☐ Four (4) Tablespoons of uncooked rice (any kind)
- ☐ One (1) Tablespoon
- ☐ One (1) Roll of Scotch Tape
- ☐ Optional – Camping Stickers

Instructions:

Step 1: Talk to your child about campfires and how they are used. Fires are used when camping to keep warm and they make a crackling sound. While sitting around a campfire telling stories or singing songs, the crackling sound from the fire will be in the background.

Step 2: Place plastic Easter eggs, uncooked rice, tablespoon, scotch tape and stickers next to the child.

Step 3: Tell them to open up the plastic eggs and fill each egg with one tablespoon of uncooked rice.

Step 4: Close the eggs once the rice is inside. An adult can tape the egg shut so the rice doesn't fall out.

Step 5: If there are stickers available, allow the child to decorate each egg with stickers.

Step 6: Place a blanket on the floor. Place the pile of ten sticks in the middle of the blanket. This is the "campfire" area. The child (or children) can sit on the blanket around the campfire.

Step 7: The adult should hold two egg shakers and the child should hold two egg shakers.

Step 8: The adult should complete the following patterns using these movements:

- "**Shake**" means "**shake one egg**"
- "**Shake two**" means "**shake both eggs**"
- "**Stop**" means **pause, don't shake any eggs**"
- "**Clap**" means to "**clap your hands together using no egg shakers.**"

A. Shake, Shake, Stop, Shake, Shake, Stop, Shake, Shake, Stop... (Continue for one minute and encourage your child to join in).

B. Shake, Shake two, Stop, Shake, Shake two, Stop, Shake, Shake two, Stop... (Continue for one minute and encourage your child to join in).

C. Shake, Shake two, Shake, Shake two, Shake, Shake two... (Continue for one minute and encourage your child to join in).

D. Shake, Shake, Shake, Shake, Stop, Shake Two, Shake Two, Shake Two, Shake Two, Stop, Shake, Shake, Shake, Shake, Stop... (Continue for one minute and encourage your child to join in).

E. Shake, Shake, Shake, Clap, Shake, Shake, Shake, Clap (continue for one minute and encourage your child to join in).

F. Now have the child come up with some patterns.

A.5 Learning Objectives

Math/Science	Language/Literacy	Problem Solving	Motor Skills
•One to One Correspondence •Introduction to Patterning •Mathematical Sequences	•Increasing Vocabulary •Using Language in Conversation	•Curiosity and Initative •Engagement and Persistence •Memory •Imitating Movements	•Fine Motor: Peeling Stickers

Notes: What did your child do well? Are there any skills they need to continue to work on?

Language Development – Growing our Vocabulary

By Completing Level 3 Activities, We will learn how to…

- o Follow three-step directions.
- o Use sentences in conversation to describe, explain or predict outcomes of real or imaginary events.
- o Initiate and engage in literacy activities.

Literacy Development – Beginning Reading and Writing

By Completing Level 3 Activities, We will learn how to..

- o Write their own name, without help.
- o Write familiar words by looking at the word then copying.
- o Identify all letters by sight and sound

B1. Tent Stories - Activity time: 15 minutes

Materials Needed
- ☐ One (1) Piece of Blank White Paper
- ☐ One (1) Yellow Highlighter
- ☐ One (1) Pen

Instructions:

Step 1: Explain to your child that sometimes at night at home, people read stories to relax. You can do the same thing in a tent.

Step 2: Explain to the child that you are going to make up a camping story together to read before bed.

Step 3: Ask your child what they would like to name their story. The name of the story is called the "title" of the story. Write down what their story title with the yellow highlighter. Make sure to use both uppercase and lowercase letters.

Step 4: Ask your child the follow questions, encouraging them to describe any story that they would like. Use a yellow highlighter to write the story down on a piece of paper.

- Who is in the story?
- What will happen?
- Where will it happen?
- When will it happen?
- Why will it happen throughout the story?

Step 5: When they're finished, read the story out loud that you wrote down on the paper.

Step 6: Give the child a pen or a pencil and encourage them to trace the words that are written (including the title of the story).

Step 7: Ask the child to write their name. If they can't write it on their own yet, you can write it in yellow highlighter and have them trace it. Tell them that the author of a book is the person who wrote the book. The author always has their name on the front of a book so other people know who wrote the story. They are the author!

Optional: Pick out some books and read who the authors are of their favorite stories.

B.1 Learning Objectives

Math/Science	Language/Literacy	Problem Solving	Motor Skills
• N/A	• Increasing Vocabulary • Write their own name, without help. • Write familiar words by looking at the word then copying. • Identify letters and words by sight and sound • Use sentences in conversation to describe, explain or predict outcomes of real or imaginary events. • Initiate and engage in literacy activities.	• Curiosity and Initative • Engagement and Persistence • Memory • Understanding the parts of a story. • Answering open-ended questions.	• Fine Motor: Copying Letters

Notes: What did your child do well? Are there any skills they need to continue to work on?

B2. In the Dark, Dark Night - Activity time: 15 minutes

Materials Needed
- ☐ One (1) Flashlight
- ☐ One (1) Piece of Blank Paper
- ☐ One (1) Black Marker
- ☐ One (1) Yellow Highlighter
- ☐ Time of day when it is dark outside

Instructions:

Step 1: Give the child a flashlight that is turned on. Explain to them that when people go camping, there is no electricity. Flashlights are used to see in the dark. When it's dark, the adult and child should go outside into a safe place. If it's not possible to go outside, then turn the lights off in your home.

Step 2: Tell the child you're going on a search for 10 items that are on the ground. Tell your child to shine the light on each object they find.

Step 3: The adult should write down the name of the items the child finds.

Step 4: Once the child has found 10 items, go back indoors and turn the flashlight off.

Step 5: Show the child the list items they found.

Step 6: Ask them to identify/name the first letter of each Item.

Step 7: Tell your child to use a yellow highlighter trace that letter with a yellow highlighter.

B.2 Learning Objectives

Math/Science	Language/Literacy	Problem Solving	Motor Skills
• One to One Correspondence • Counting to 10	• Increasing Vocabulary o Write familiar words by looking at the word then copying. o Identify all letters by sight and sound o Follow Directions	• Curiosity and Initative • Engagement and Persistence • Memory • Opposites	• Fine Motor: Using a highlighter to write/trace letters.

Notes: What did your child do well? Are there any skills they need to continue to work on?

B3. Going on a Bear Hunt - Activity time: 25 minutes

Materials Needed
☐ One (1) blank piece of white paper
☐ One (1) set of markers or crayons
☐ Access to the internet

Instructions:

Step 1: Tell the child you're going to watch a video of one of the Authors who wrote the book, **"We Are Going On a Bear Hunt"**, tell the story. Ask them if they remember what an author is from activity B.1 (Tent Stories)?

Step 2: Watch the YouTube video: <u>We Are Going on a Bear Hunt</u> by Michal Rosen
https://www.youtube.com/watch?v=0gyl6ykDwds

Step 3: Ask your child to name all the things the people had to do on the bear hunt.

Step 4: Watch the video again telling the child to listen for all of the obstacles the people had to overcome while going on the bear hunt.

Step 5: Ask the child if they can tell you what happened in the story.

Step 6: Fold a piece of paper in half then fold it in half again. Fold the paper in half one more time.

Step 7: Open the piece of paper and draw a line down each of the creases with a pen. There should be eight sections when done.

Step 8: Number each box (1 through 8) by writing the number on the top right corner of each box. Write each "obstacle" in the bottom of each box in the order it occurred:

1) Home
2) Grass
3) River
4) Mud
5) Forest
6) Snowstorm
7) A Cave
8) Home

1	2	3	4
Home	Grass	River	Mud
5	6	7	8
Forrest	Snowstorm	A Cave	Home

Step 9: Using Markers or Crayons, tell the child to draw a picture of the "obstacle" in each box.

> **Example**: Draw grass in the box labeled "grass", a river in the box labeled "river" and so on.

Step 10: Ask your child to trace the numbers written in each grid, naming each number as they trace it.

Step 11: Ask your child to trace the words written in each grid, naming each letter as they trace it.

Optional: Watch the video again, asking the child act it out the motions in the video.

B.3 Learning Objectives

Math/Science	Language/Literacy	Problem Solving	Motor Skills
•Categorizing •Number Identification	•Increasing Vocabulary •Write their own name, without help. •Identify letters by sight and sound •Follow directions. •Use sentences in conversation to describe, explain or predict outcomes of real or imaginary events. •Initiate and engage in literacy activities. •Comprehension of text	•Curiosity and Initative •Engagement and Persistence •Memory •Immitating Movements	•Fine Motor: Using crayons to copy letters and numbers

Notes: What did your child do well? Are there any skills they need to continue to work on?

B4. Camping Word Bank - Activity time: 15 minutes

Materials Needed
- One (1) Yellow highlighter
- One (1) Pen
- One (1) Piece of blank, white paper
- One (1) Black marker

Instructions:

Step 1: On a blank piece of white paper, the adult should write the following questions with a pen or marker:

1) What do you sleep in?

2) What keeps your warm?

3) What do you eat?

4) What do you drink?

5) Where do you go?

6) What do you see with when it gets dark?

7) What keeps the bugs away?

8) How do you brush your teeth?

9) What do you wear?

10) How do you carry things when hiking?

Step 2: Ask the child the questions and write down their answers with a yellow highlighter.

Step 3: Encourage the child to trace the words written in yellow highlighter with a pen or pencil.

B.4 Learning Objectives

Math/Science	Language/Literacy	Problem Solving	Motor Skills
• N/A	• Increasing Vocabulary • Write familiar words by looking at the word then copying. • Identify all letters by sight and sound • Use sentences in conversation to describe, explain or predict outcomes of real or imaginary events. • Answer open-ended questions	• Memory	• Fine Motor: Using a pen to trace letters.

Notes: What did your child do well? Are there any skills they need to continue to work on?

B5. Stick Name - Activity time: 15 minutes

Materials Needed
- ☐ One (1) Piece of Blank Piece of Construction Paper, Any Color
- ☐ One (1) Bottle of Elmer's Glue
- ☐ One (1) Black Marker
- ☐ Ten (10) Skinny sticks (Fallen sticks from trees)

Instructions:

Step 1: Go outdoors, near trees, with the child and help them find ten skinny sticks that have fallen onto the ground.

Step 3: Return to your home and use a black marker to write the child's name in uppercase letters on the blank piece of construction paper.

Step 4: If they're able, allow the child to trace the letters with the bottle of Elmer's Glue. If they're not yet able to trace with the glue, have an adult do it.

Step 5: Next, have the child break the sticks into small pieces and place them onto the glue. Place their stick name in a spot to dry.

B.5 Learning Objectives

Math/Science	Language/Literacy	Problem Solving	Motor Skills
•Number Sense •Quantity and Counting	•Increasing Vocabulary •Letter and Word Knowledge •Concepts of Print •Write familiar words by looking at the word then copying. •Follow directions.	•Curiosity and Initative •Engagement and Persistence	•Fine Motor: Using Glue to Trace Letters

Notes: What did your child do well? Are there any skills they need to continue to work on?

Gross Motor – Using our large muscles to move!

By Completing Level 3 Activities, We will learn…

- o **Participate in a variety of gross motor activities that require balance and coordination.**
- o **Hop on one foot five or more times.**

Fine Motor – Using our hands to complete tasks

By Completing Level 3 Activities, We will learn…

- o **Use scissors to cut out an object.**
- o **Use a pen or marker to write familiar words.**
- o **Use a pencil to trace new words.**

C1. Tracing Nature - Activity time: 15 minutes

Materials Needed
☐ One (1) Bucket or Plastic Bag
☐ Three (3) Pieces of White Construction Paper
☐ One (1) Set of Markers or Colored Pencils
☐ Access to an Outdoor Environment

Instructions:

Step 1: Tell the child you are going to go on a scavenger hunt.

Step 2: Give them a bucket or an empty bag and tell to collect 20 natural objects they find outside. These can include sticks, shells, leaves, rocks, etc.

Step 3: Tell the child to count the objects, one by one, to make sure they have 20.

Step 4: Return indoors and encourage the child to place the objects onto a table, and sort them into piles that are **similar.** For example: Put all of the leaves together in one pile then place the sticks together in one pile and so on.

Step 5: Once the items are sorted, have the child count how many items are in each pile.

Step 6: Write the name of one item the child found on one piece of blank paper.

Step 7: Write the number of items that are in that pile, next to the words you wrote for Step 6. For example: If there are **three leaves,** write the **number 3** on the sheet of paper that has the word **"leaf"** on it.

Step 8: Repeat Step 6 and 7 until all items are written down.

Step 9: Tell the child to use colored pencils to trace each object on the corresponding paper. For example: All leaves should be traced on the piece of paper that has the word "leaf" written on it.

Step 10: Tell the child to count each traced item.

Step 11: Use a pen to trace the words and numbers written in yellow highlighter.

C1. Learning Objectives

Math/Science	Language/Literacy	Problem Solving	Motor Skills
• Number Sense • Quantity and Counting • Counting to 20	• Increasing Vocabulary • Letter and Word Knowledge • Concepts of Print • Tracing Words • Follow directions.	• Memory and Knowledge • Engagement and Persistence • Exploration • Sorting and Classification	• Fine Motor: Tracing Letters and Numbers • Fine Motor: Tracing Objects • Gross Motor: Walking and seaching for items

Notes: What did your child do well? Are there any skills they need to continue to work on?

C2. Edible Tent - Activity time: 15 minutes

Materials Needed
- ☐ Eight (8) to Ten (10) Pretzel Sticks
- ☐ One (1) Tablespoon of Peanut Butter or Cream Cheese
- ☐ One (1) Graham Cracker Square
- ☐ One (1) Pen
- ☐ One (1) Piece of Blank White Paper
- ☐ One (1) Piece of Blank Lined Paper
- ☐ One (1) Plastic knife

Instructions:

Step 1: Place all materials in front of the child.

Step 2: Tell them that they are going to make an edible tent.

Step 3: Have the child use a plastic knife to spread the Peanut Butter OR Cream Cheese onto the Graham Cracker Square.

Step 4: Tell the child to place all of the pretzel sticks onto the Peanut Butter or Cream Cheese, with one end in the cream cheese and the other end in the air (standing straight up vertically).

Step 5: Can the child figure out how to stop the pretzel sticks from falling over?

> **Answer:** The pretzel stick ends, in the air, must meet together in the middle, to gain support by leaning on each other.

Step 6: Encourage the child to use crayons to draw a picture of the edible tent they just made.

Step 7: Ask the child to create a story about the tent they made. The adult should use a pen to write down what the child says. Ask your child the following questions to help create their story:

- Who lives in it?
- Where is the family camping at?
- What adventure are they going on?

Step 8: Once the story is complete, allow the child to eat the edible tent they made. The adult should read the story back to the child while they are eating.

Step 9: Ask the child write their name on the top of the story, to signify he/she is the author.

C2. Learning Objectives

Math/Science	Language/Literacy	Problem Solving	Motor Skills
•N/A	•Increasing Vocabulary •Letter and Word Knowledge •Use Words •Follow directions. •Creating Stories •Answering Open-Ended Questions.	•Memory and Knowledge •Engagement and Persistence	•Fine Motor: Using Pens to Write •Fine Motor: Balance

Notes: What did your child do well? Are there any skills they need to continue to work on?

C3. Direction Obstacle Course - Activity time: 30 minutes

Materials Needed
- ☐ Four (4) Pillows
- ☐ Large Indoor or Outdoor Space
- ☐ One (1) Large Cardboard Box or Empty Laundry Basket
- ☐ One (1) Hula Hoop
- ☐ One (1) Jump Rope
- ☐ One (1) Timer

Instructions:

Step 1: Place all of the items from the materials list around a large open space. Tell the child that when they get to each item, they must complete a different action. Use the following action key to explain what the child should do when they get to each object:

- ○ Pillows – Jump Over
- ○ Hula Hoop – Crawl through
- ○ Jump Rope – Walk on a Straight Line
- ○ Cardboard Box/Empty Laundry Basket – Climb in and Climb Out

Step 2: There are lots of obstacles when camping, including barriers to climb over, tree limbs to duck under and skinny trails to walk on. These obstacles will provide practice to learn body awareness, a skill needed to avoid obstacles in the woods.

Step 3: The adult should demonstrate completing the course first using the actions in Step 1.

Step 4: Ready, Set, Go! Time the child to see how fast they can complete the obstacle course. Can they do it faster the second time?

C3. Learning Objectives

Math/Science	Language/Literacy	Problem Solving	Motor Skills
•N/A	•Follow multi-step directions. •New Vocabulary	•Memory and Knowledge •Engagement and Persistence	•Gross Motor: Jumping, Running, Body Awareness, Coordination

Notes: What did your child do well? Are there any skills they need to continue to work on?

C4. Tree-Tag - Activity time: 20 minutes

Materials Needed
- ☐ One large park where there are trees
- ☐ One (1) Bucket or Bag
- ☐ One (1) Timer

Instructions:

Step 1: Find an area close by which has a lot of trees. Tell the child it's their job to collect as many leaves as they can in one minute.

Step 2: Give them a small bucket or bag to place the leaves into.

Step 3: Set the timer for one minute and tell the child to come back when the buzzer goes off.

Step 4: When the child returns, help them count the leaves they found. Placing them into a pile.

Step 5: Repeat steps 3 and 4. This time when the child comes back, count how many leaves they found the **second time**. Did they find **more or less leaves** than they found the first time?

Step 6: What is the difference between the amount of leaves the child found? Step 7 and 8 explain how to help the child subtract the larger number from the smaller number.

Step 7: Place the first set of leaves in a horizontal line.

Step 8: Place the second collection of leaves in a horizontal line, directly under the first line.

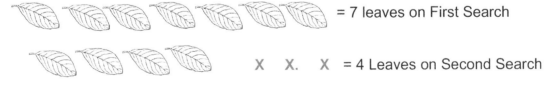

= 7 leaves on First Search

X   X.   X   = 4 Leaves on Second Search

3 Leaves Less

Ask the child the following questions:

- Which line has more leaves?
- How many more leaves are there in the longer line?
- How many leaves to we add to the lines to make them the same?

C4. Learning Objectives

Math/Science	Language/Literacy	Problem Solving	Motor Skills
• One to One Correspondence • Mathematical Operations • Compare and Contrast	• Follow Multi-Step Directions • New Vocabulary	• Memory and Knowledge • Engagement and Persistence	• Gross Motor: Running, Body Awareness, Coordination

Notes: What did your child do well? Are there any skills they need to continue to work on?

✎ C5. Spider Web Jump - Activity time: 15 minutes

Materials Needed
☐ One (1) Stick of Sidewalk Chalk
☐ One (1) Outside Concrete Area

Instructions:

Step 1: Tell the child there are a lot of different types of bugs when you go camping. For this game, you are both going to pretend you are spiders and you're investigating your web (home).

Step 2: On a large area of concrete, using the sidewalk chalk, draw a large circle - **at least four feet in diameter.**

Step 3: Inside the circle, draw a variety of lines that intersect with each other. Make sure there is enough room for the child to step between each line.

Step 4: Tell the child that they are "jumping" spiders and it's their job to jump over the lines in their web.

Step 5: Tell the child that he/she **should try not to step or jump on the lines**. Instead, they **should jump over the lines**.

Step 6: Tell them you're going to sing a jumping song. When you say **"stop",** they should **freeze** until you start singing again.

Step 7: The adult should clap their hands and chant or sing the following words:

Jumping Song

Jumping, jumping, jumping,

Jumping, jumping, jumping,

Jumping, jumping, jumping,

Jumping, Jumping, STOP!

Step 7: When you stay "STOP", stop clapping and freeze. The child should freeze at this time also.

Step 8: Repeat step number 6 and 7. Continue for as long as desired.

C5. Learning Objectives

Math/Science	Language/Literacy	Problem Solving	Motor Skills
• N/A	• Follow Multi-Step Directions • New Vocabulary	• Understanding Visual and Auditor Cues • Engagement and Persistence	• Gross Motor: Jumping, Body Awareness, Coordination

Notes: What did your child do well? Are there any skills they need to continue to work on?

Themed Project – Outdoor Exploration

Purpose: To teach the process of finding answers to new questions. Each project guides adults and children through investigating specific questions about the theme. The project starts with the development of a hypothesis that is then tested and researched, concluding with an answer to the hypothesis. Specific Learning Objectives include:

Problem Solving Skills: By Completing Level 3, We will learn…

- o **Predict the results of a familiar action.**
- o **Develop strategies to solve a problem.**
- o **Communicate memories about a sequence of related events that happened in the past.**
- o **Put materials or objects together in new and inventive ways.**
- o **Participate in challenging multi-step activities/projects**
- o **Demonstrate Curiosity and ask Questions.**
- o **Use words to discuss predictions.**
- o **Use language to reiterate process and conclusions.**
- o **Use a variety of techniques to record information and data collection.**

Includes: Activities and discussions that address all areas of academic and developmental skills that meets the Level 3 Learning Objectives. Includes math, science, literacy, art, health/safety, gross motor skills, fine motor skills, music and movement and literacy development.

Order of Operation: These projects are designed to be followed in the order they are laid out, each activity building on the knowledge acquired from previous activities.

Project Objective:

When this project is completed, your child should be able to answer the question:

What do you need in order to survive in the Wilderness?

Introduction Activity:

Materials Needed
- Two (2) Sheets of Blank Paper
- One (1) Box of Crayons or Markers
- One (1) Yellow Highlighter (or any other color)
- One (1) Pen

Instructions:

Step 1: Ask your child to draw a picture of a typical campsite.

Step 2: Review the photo with your child. Ask them what each item is and why they included it.

Step 3: The adult should use a yellow highlighter to write down what the child says on a blank piece of paper.

Step 4: Ask your child to trace the words with a pen.

Investigation

Section 1: Living Outdoors

Activity #1 – Camping Food Investigation

Materials Needed
- One (1) or two (2) different grocery store sale papers
- One (1) Pair of Child-sized scissors
- One (1) Blank Piece of Paper (any kind and color)
- One (1) Glue Stick
- One (1) Pen

Instructions:

Step 1: Ask the child the following question: When people go camping, most don't have a refrigerator or stove. What kind of food could you bring to a place like that?

Step 2: Listen to what they have to say.

Step 3: Tell them there are lots of different types of foods that can be used.

Step 4: Tell the child you are going to look through the sale paper together to find items you would need to go camping.

Step 5: When the child finds items that can be used for camping food and materials, encourage them to use child-safe scissors to cut them out (these could include paper products, food items such as breads, cereal bars, items to roast over the fire, water jugs, etc).

Step 6: Have the child glue the items onto a piece of paper with a glue stick.

Step 7: Ask the child to name each item. The adult should write the name of the items under their corresponding picture.

Activity #2: Developing a Camping Area

Step 1: Ask the child the following question: What items do we need to take when we go camping?

Step 2: Listen to what they have to say.

Step 3: Tell you kids that tonight you're going to have a family campout! The child will need to gather everything they need to take if they were really going on a camping trip.

Step 4: Review the photo they drew in Activity #1. Collect everything from that list and place them in the center of one room. Some suggestions of items are:

- o Blankets and pillows for makeshift sleeping bags (or regular sleeping bags)
- o A tarp
- o Bug Spray
- o Toothbrush and toiletries
- o Warm clothes
- o Anything else they put on the list

Step 5: Watch a video about how to set up a campsite. There are quite a few on the internet. One wonderful Video is called:

How To Setup a Campsite by Howtodo Florida TV

https://www.youtube.com/watch?v=yu3E4oMqG_0

Step 6: After watching the video suggested in Discussion #2, ask the child what steps he/she remembers from the video?

Examples include: Check in office, Quiet hours, Shade, Fire area, Sleeping area, Washing area, Raccoon box/Bear box, Water tank, Flashlights, etc.)

Step 7: Now go on a search either inside or outside of your home, for the perfect "campsite" that the child will be able to sleep tonight (with an adult).

Step 8: Once the "campsite" is found, set up camp! Utilize the camping materials the child found in Step 3. Is there anything you forgot? Does the child remember the important components of a campsite from the How To Setup a Campsite Video?

Step 9: The campout night has begun! Sing songs listed on the song list **(in Appendix A),** eat camping "snacks" and read camping books. Most importantly, have fun making memories.

**Note - Since using fire in a residential area is extremely dangerous, parents can put a pile of flashlights in the middle of the "fire ring".

Activity #3: Caring for the Environment

Step 1: The next "morning", when your "evening" of camping has come to an end, tell the child that it's very important that everyone helps clean up the campsite to make sure the animals living in the environment have a clean place to live.

Step 2: Encourage the child to help pack all of the items they brought to camp and put them back where they belong.

Step 3: Using a trash bag, have the child roam around the "camping" area and pick up all of the trash from the "night before". It's important to always leave a campsite in the same condition that you found it (or even cleaner than you found it).

Step 4: Ask the child what their favorite part of the camping night was and what they would do differently next time.

Section 2: Sharing Our World

Activity #4: Raccoon Boxes - Activity time: 30 minutes

Materials Needed
- One (1) Empty Shoe Box
- One (1) Package of Markers or Crayons
- One (1) Black Marker
- Three (3) Blank Pieces of White Paper
- Access to the internet

Instructions:

Step 1: Raccoons love to eat food! When humans go camping, it's important for them to keep their food locked up so that raccoons and other animals don't eat it.

Step 2: If the child doesn't know what a raccoon is, or has never seen one, look for a video of photo of raccoons on the internet. One example is the following YouTube video:

> Baby Racoons Stealing Pizza by Taya Baldridge:
> **https://www.youtube.com/watch?v=pfwr-mYVJiw**

Step 3: After watching the video, ask your child if they think Raccoons would eat our food if it was left it out?

Step 4: Ask the child to use a piece of paper and markers or crayons to draw the following foods:
1. Five cookies
2. Four Apples
3. Three chips
4. Two Pieces of Bread
5. One piece of Pizza

Step 5: Ask your child to count **the total amount** of each type of food. Encourage them to point to each piece when they say each number.

Step 6: Ask them the following questions:

- What food is there the **most** of (Answer: 5 cookies)?
- Which type of food has the **least** amount of (Answer: 1 piece of pizza)?

Step 7: Have your child use child-safe scissors to cut out each food item they drew.

Step 8: Tell them the raccoons will come eat the food if it isn't hidden in the raccoon box when you go camping. Tell the child to put all the pieces of food into the shoebox.

Step 9: The adult should use a black marker to write the word "Raccoon Box" on the shoebox. Allow your child to use the "Raccoon Box" in the pretend play/ dramatic play area of your home.

Activity #5: Ants on a Log - Activity time: 15 minutes

Materials Needed
- One (1) Piece of Washed Celery (not cut)
- Two (2) Tablespoons of Peanut Butter or Cream Cheese
- Ten (10) Raisins
- One (1) Plastic Knife

Instructions:

Step 1: Put one piece of celery, two spoonfuls of peanut butter, one plastic knife and ten raisins on a plate.

Step 2: Tell your child to use the plastic knife to spread the peanut butter on the celery (log).

Step 3: Now have the child place the ten raisins (ants) on the log in a row.

Step 4: Ask the child to count the raisins by pointing to each raisin.

Step 5: Ask the child to eat one raisin then repeat step 4. Have them repeat the phrase:

"(Ten) raisins minus (take away) one makes (nine) raisins".

Step 6: Repeat steps 4 and 5 until all of the raisins have been eaten.

Step 7: Allow the child to eat the celery stick.

Step 8: If desired, repeat the activity with up to twenty raisins.

Activity #6: Fishing Patterns - Activity time: 20 minutes

Materials Needed
- Access to the Internet
- One (1) Ruler
- One (1) Black Marker
- One (1) Box of Crayons
- One (3) Sheets of Sturdy Construction Paper (any color)
- One (1) Pair of Adult scissors
- One (1) Long Stick or branch
- One (1) Roll of Scotch Tape

Instructions:

Step 1: Today, we're going to go fishing! Tell the child there are lots of different types of fish, even ones with different sizes and colors.

Step 2: Show the child the ruler. Explain to them that each number represents **one inch**. Using a black pen and the construction paper, draw three, one-inch lines.

Step 3: Draw three lines, each two inches long.

Step 4: Draw three lines, each three inches long.

Step 5: The one-inch lines are "**little**", the two-inch lines are "**medium**" and the three-inch lines are "**big**".

Step 6: The parent should use the maker to draw a fish on each line. See picture:

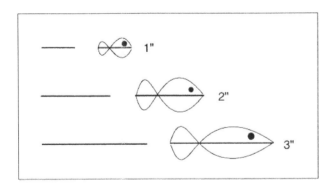

Step 7: The adult should cut each fish out and place them on the floor.
    ***Optional**: Put a hula hoop or an empty baby pool on the floor and place the fish inside.

Step 8: Tell the child it's time to go "fishing"! Take a walk around your neighborhood or backyard to find a stick that would be a good "fishing pole".

Step 9: The adult should place a rounded piece of scotch tape on the top of each fish.

Step 10: Encourage the child to go fishing! They should use their stick to poke the part of the fish that has tape on it in order to "pull up the fish".

Step 11: Encourage the child to sort the fish they "catch" by category:

- Small fish
- Medium fish
- Big fish

Step 12: Repeat steps 8 though 10 as many times as desired.

*Optional: Can the child use the fish they caught to make a pattern? For Example:

Small fish, medium fish, large fish, small fish, medium fish, large fish, etc.

Activity #7: Footprint Classification - Activity time: 20 minutes

Materials Needed
- One (1) Bucket of Water (small amount)
- One (1) Stick of Sidewalk Chalk
  - Optional: Internet Access
  - Optional: Wet Sand

Instructions:

Step 1: Talk to the child about what they see on the ground outside. There are lot of things on the ground and lots of footprints.

> *** Optional:** View a variety of different animal tracks here:
> https://www.pinterest.com/explore/animal-tracks/

Step 2: Fill a bucket with no more than two cups of water. Place the bucket on a concrete surface.

Step 3: Make sure the child has bare feet. Tell them to step into the bucket and then step onto the concrete. Can they see their wet footprint?

Step 4: Tell the child to use sidewalk chalk to trace their wet footprint.

Step 5: Have an adult (with bare feet) step into the bucket and step out. Do you see the adults' footprints? Make sure the adult doesn't walk on the child's footprint!

Step 6: Have the child trace the adult footprints with the sidewalk chalk.

Step 7: Ask the child:
- Which footprint is big?
- Which footprint is small?

Step 8: Have the child use a ruler to count how many inches long their footprint is. Write the number, using the chalk, next to their footprint.

Step 9: Tell them to count how many inches the adult footprint is. Write the number, using the chalk, next to the adult's footprint.

---

* Optional: Place wet sand on a baking tray. Put the tray on the ground and encourage the child to walk, with bare feet, from the pavement to the sand then off of the sand.

- Can they see the footprint they made in the sand?
- Encourage them to measure the footprints.
- Can they see their toes in the sand?
- How many toes can they see?

Section 3: Outdoor Safety

Activity #8. Camping Solutions - Activity time: 30 minutes

Materials Needed
- One large outdoor space that is kid-friendly
- Access to the internet
- Timer on a phone or a watch

Step 1: Explain the following to your child:

When camping, it's always important to stay near our adults and family. If for some reason, a child finds that they have wandered too far, it's important to stop, find a tree and stay in one spot. The National Association for Search and Rescue has made an instructional video for children, showing them what to do if they find themselves lost in the forest.

Step 2: Tell the child they are going to watch a video on how to be safe when camping in the forest.

Step 3: Watch the following video on "Hug a Tree": Created by Southern CA Rescue Teams
https://www.youtube.com/watch?v=I6P9ugnf2Nc

Step 4: After watching the video, talk to the child about what it means to "hug a tree". Tell them that if they don't know where they are, they should find a tree to stay at until help arrives.

Step 5: Go outside, near tree-filled area.

Step 6: Tell the child you are going to play "hug a tree".

Step 7: Set a timer for thirty seconds. Tell the child to find a bush or a tree and sit next to it.

Step 8: When the timer goes off, the adult should find the child and give them a "high-five" for hugging a tree and staying there.

Step 9: Now switch roles. Have the adult go find a tree and then tell the child to come find you.

Step 10: Repeat steps 6 through 8 for at least five minutes

Conclusion

Activity #9: Memory

Step 1: Using the markers/crayons and a blank sheet of white paper, ask the child to draw a picture of your family camping night from activity in Activity #2: A Night For Camping.

Step 2: Once the child has completed their picture, ask them to tell you a story about what happened the night you went camping.

Step 3: Using a pen and paper, write down what the child says. Keep this picture and story for memories for years to come.

Activity #10: Knowledge

Step 1: Ask your child the following questions:

- What types of animals live in the world?
- Where do fish live?
- Why should we keep our world clean?
- What happens if you can't find an adult? What should you do?
- What do you think is the most important thing to have when you go camping?

Step 2: Ask your child if there is anything else they want to know about the outdoors and camping?

Step 3: Write down their questions and help them look for the answers!

Suggested Camping Songs

'Going Camping'
By Author Unknown

Sung to: "I'm a Little Teapot"
I am going camping.
(point thumbs proudly to chest)
Time to pack
(point to wristwatch)
My tent, my bedroll,
(Make tent with hands; then fold hands to cheek.)
And a snack.
(Pretend to eat)
I'll sit by the campfire
(warm hands over fire.)
Its glow so bright.
(Fan and wiggle fingers to resemble fire.)
Then snooze in my tent
(Pretend to snore.)
'Till the morning light!
(Open eyes wide, forming sun overhead.)

'Twinkle Twinkle'
By Author Unknown

Twinkle, twinkle little star;
How I wonder what you are.
Up above the world so high
Like a diamond in the sky.
Twinkle, twinkle little star;
How I wonder what you are.

'A Camping We Will Go'
By Barney

A Camping we will go
A Camping we will go
Hi Ho the dairy o!
A Camping we will go
We fix the tent right here
We fix the tent right here
Hi Ho the dairy o!
We fix the tent right here
We crawling to the tent
We crawling to the tent
Hi Ho the dairy o!
We crawling to the tent
We're having lots of fun!
We're having lots of fun!
Hi Ho the dairy o!

. . . .

Thanks for playing! See you in the next Unit:
Pre-K Your Way - Level 3, Unit 2
Transportation: Package Delivery Systems.

Pre-K YOUR Way

Level 3 Unit 2

Transportation
Package Delivery Systems Project

Transportation Themed Items For Indoor Learning Environment

Now that you have set up your environment, you are ready to place materials in it that directly relate to the theme you are studying! Here are some suggestions of materials your child can free-play with during the "Exploring My Community" Theme:

Books: Age-appropriate books that directly correlate with the monthly theme can be found at your local library or bought separately online. This is a great opportunity to take a trip with your child to your local library and go on a search together. Have them identify words or pictures on the cover of children's books that correlate to the theme. Place a variety of books related to the theme in your child's book area. This will increase opportunities for them to expand their knowledge and use what they learn in the activities to comprehend what they read in the books.

These are age-appropriate books that directly correlate with the monthly theme, which can be found at your local library or bought separately online.

1. Transportation in Many Cultures (Life Around the World) – by Martha E. H. Rustad

2. National Geographic Little Kids Look and Learn: Things That Go – by National Geographic Kids

3. If I Built A Car – by Chris Van Dusen

4. My Truck is Stuck – by Kevin Lewis

5. The Goodnight Train– by June Sobel and Laura Huliska-Beith

6. Sheep in a Jeep – by Nancey E. Shaw and Margot Apple

7. The Little Engine That Could – by Watty Piper

Art Area: Encourage your child use this throughout each day by rotating items in an art area. These can be items have already been painted on, paper that they drew on already or leftover materials from another project. Thought provoking art projects are created when children are given unlimited opportunities to explore a variety of materials.

Some suggestions for the art area include:
- Crayons
- Paper
- Pens
- Empty Boxes (all kinds)
- Empty Toilet Paper or Paper Towel Rolls
- Foil
- Clean Q-tips for painting
- Scraps of paper
- Scraps of Yarn
- Scraps of any type of material – including fabric, sand paper, etc.
- Paper Bags
- Straws
- Popsicle Sticks
- Anything else that can be reused.

Suggested Cooking Activities:

These are simple cooking and snack-time activities that correlate with the theme. The children can prepare these snacks with adult assistance.

1) **Train Color Snack:** Ask the child to place six graham cracker halves in a line. Next, tell them that this train is going to carry six different colors of freight. Using a spoon, place one teaspoon of cream cheese on each graham cracker half. Using food coloring, have the child place one drop of each color on its own graham cracker. Using a spoon, mix the food color into the cream cheese. Next, have the child name what each train car color is. Have them sound out the name of the color and see if they can say what letter each color starts with. Time to eat!

2) **My Family Car:** Have the child place a piece of bread on a plate. Next, have them count out four circle crackers. Place the crackers at the bottom of the plate to make the wheels. Next, encourage the child to use a toothpick to cut lines in the bread where they would put a windows and doors in the car. The adult can help the child take out the windows that the child outlined with the toothpick. Time to eat!

Sensory Bin Suggestions

A sensory bin is a small plastic bucket that is filled with a variety of materials. Sensory bins provide a space to engage in sensory-rich activities that offer opportunities to investigate textures while providing activities for relaxation and self-regulation. Sensory bins encourage language development, small motor development and control, spatial concepts, problem-solving skills and scientific observations. Each month there are suggested sensory bin materials that correlate with the theme of the unit.

Set Up Instructions: In a Plastic Bucket, rotate the following sensory activities throughout the month.

1. **Sand Writing Table:**

   Mix 2 cups of sand, 1 ½ cups cold water and 1 cup of cornstarch together. Stir the mixture for five to ten minutes over medium heat until it becomes thick. Pour the thick sand onto a cookie sheet. After it cools, have your child practice writing the Letter of the Week, Number of the Week and drawing the Shape of the Week in the sand.
       Note: You can also use this mixture to build sand castles that will stick together longer.

2. *Water investigation (Washing the car):*

   Place water, two tablespoons of Dawn dish soap, sponges and plastic cars into a sensory bin. Allow the child to wash all of the cars using the items in the bin. Once they are clean, help them dry the items with a towel.

3. **Tracks Painting:**

   Place a variety of different toy cars, trucks and airplanes into a sensory bin. Place piece of foil on the bottom of the sensory bin and add two tablespoons of finger paint. Allow the child to dip the different transportation items into the paint and "drive" them across the foil. When finished, ask them if they can they identify the tracks that each item made?

Dramatic Play Area

This play area allows children to understand and experience the adult world through imitation and creativity. The dramatic play area provides a safe space for young children to create stories while practicing new vocabulary and practicing social skills. It is also a space where groups of children engage in pretend play which provides opportunities to learn self-help skills, share space and materials, take turns and the use abstract thinking. Each month there is a list of suggested materials to integrate into this area, which correlate with the theme of the month.

Suggested props to include in the dramatic play/pretend play area include:

- Plastic Planes
- Child – sized chairs
- Play Money (Monopoly)
- Suitcases
- Small pieces of paper (tickets)
- Books about Airplanes/Helicopters and Airports
- Pictures of real airplanes
- Books about Trains and Train stations
- Pictures of Trains
- Books about Buses and Bus Stations
- Pictures of Buses
- Pictures of Family Members cars
- Pictures of Horseback Riders

Learning Objectives - Level 3

After completing all modules in the Level 3 Curriculum Series, the child should be able to:

Mathematics
- o Solve simple addition and subtractions problems with objects.
- o Count up to 20 objects, using one to one correspondence.
- o Recognizes the names of Numerals.
- o Understands size words (Smaller vs. Larger).
- o Describe shapes by at least two characteristics.
- o Complete patterns that have two or more elements.
- o Sort objects into groups by two or more attributes.
- o Show understanding of measurement by using measuring tools.

Science
- o Demonstrate Curiosity and ask Questions
- o Engage in problem solving techniques.
- o Use words to discuss predictions
- o Use language to reiterate process and conclusions
- o Use a variety of techniques to record information and data collection
- o Use language to describe objects by a variety of attributes
- o Demonstrate understanding of differences between people, animals, plants and other parts of the planet.
- o Complete multi-step projects.

Language and Literacy
- o Write their own name, without help.
- o Follow three-step directions.
- o Use sentences in conversation to describe, explain or predict outcomes of real or imaginary events.
- o Initiate and engage in literacy activities.
- o Write familiar words by looking at the word then copying.
- o Identify all letters by sight and sound

Problem Solving Skills
- o Predict the results of a familiar action.
- o Develop strategies to solve a problem.
- o Communicate memories about a sequence of related events that happened in the past.
- o Put materials or objects together in new and inventive ways.
- o Participate in challenging multi-step activities.

Gross Motor/Fine Motor Development
- o Participate in a variety of gross motor activities that require balance and coordination.
- o Hop on one foot five or more times.
- o Use scissors to cut out an object.
- o Use a pen or marker to write familiar words.
- o Use a pencil to trace new words

Part 1: Transportation Themed Activities

These activities have been developed to meet specific, age-appropriate, Kindergarten-Readiness skills. These skills are specified in the learning objectives of each activity. The following activities may be completed in any order desired and are specifically designed to address the academic domains: math, science, language, literacy, cognitive, problem solving, and physical development.

Each activity is on its own page. If the adult chooses to print the activities, the space below each activity is provided for adults to write notes regarding the activity. Adults are encouraged to note if the child enjoyed the activity and if the child needs to work on specific learning objectives. Each activity can be repeated more than once to enable the child to master the learning objectives designed for that activity.

A. Math/Science Development

1. Wheel Shapes
2. Delivery Please
3. Cars and Trucks
4. Unicycles vs. Bicycles
5. The Gas Station

B. Language/Literacy Development

1. Helicopter Ride
2. The Great Big Car
3. The Little Me that Could
4. Red, Green and Yellow
5. Driven Name

C. Physical Development- Gross Motor & Fine-Motor

1. Wheel Rolling
2. Practice Rides
3. My Own Two Feet
4. Horseback Riding and other Animal Friends
5. Tire Jump

Mathematical Development – Understanding Numbers and their Purpose

By Completing Level 3 Activities, We will learn how to...

- o Solve simple addition and subtractions problems with objects.
- o Count up to 20 objects, using one to one correspondence.
- o Recognizes the names of Numerals.
- o Understands size words (Smaller vs. Larger).
- o Describe shapes by at least two characteristics.
- o Complete patterns that have two or more elements.
- o Sort objects into groups by two or more attributes.
- o Show understanding of measurement by using measuring tools.

Science/Cognitive Development – Learning How to Solve Problems

By Completing Level 3 Activities, We will learn how to..

- o Demonstrate Curiosity and ask Questions
- o Engage in problem solving techniques.
- o Use words to discuss predictions
- o Use language to reiterate process and conclusions
- o Use a variety of techniques to record information and data collection
- o Use language to describe objects by a variety of attributes
- o Demonstrate understanding of differences between people, animals, plants and other parts of the planet.
- o Complete multi-step projects.

A1. Wheel Shapes - Activity time: 15 minutes

Materials Needed
☐ One (1) Object in the shape of a triangle
☐ One (1) Object in the in the shape of a circle
☐ One (1) Object in the shape of a square
☐ One (1) Blank piece of white paper.
☐ One (1) Pen

Instructions:

Step 1: Using a pen, divide a piece of blank paper into three equal sections by drawing two vertical lines, six inches apart from each other.

Step 2: The adult should draw one **triangle** in the first section.

Step 3: The adult should draw one **square** in the second section.

Step 4: The adult should draw one **circle** in the third section.

Step 5: Tell the child you're going to investigate the shape of a wheel and how it rolls.

Step 6: Ask the child to look through your home for one object that's in the **shape of a triangle**. Once they find it, ask them if they think it would make a good **wheel.** Why?

Step 7: If possible, have the child try to **roll the triangle object** to the adult **across the floor**. Did it work? If it did not work, ask your child to explain why they think this shape won't roll.

Step 8: Have the child look through your home for one object that's in the **shape of a square**. Once they find it, ask them if they think it would make a good **wheel.** Why?

Step 9: If possible, have the child try to **roll the square object** to the adult **across the floor**. Did it work? If it did not work, ask your child to explain why they think this shape won't roll.

Step 10: Have the child look through your home for one object that's in the **shape of a circle**. Once they find it, ask them if they think it would make a good **wheel.** Why?

Step 11: If possible, have the child try to **roll the circle object** to the adult **across the floor**. Did it work? Ask your child to explain why this shape would roll but the others would not.

Step 12: Show the child the piece of paper with all of the shapes drawn on it (from Step 4).

Step 13: Ask the child to circle the shape that will roll like a wheel.

Step 14: Ask the child:

- "Why does the circle with roll?"
- "How many sides does the circle have?"
- "How many corners does it have?"

Step 15: Now ask the child to identify the other shapes. Ask them the following questions:

- "Why does this shape not roll?"
- "How many sides does it have?"
- "How many corners does it have?"

A.1 Learning Objectives

Math/Science	Language/Literacy	Problem Solving	Motor Skills
•Describe shapes by at least two characteristics.	•Use sentences in conversation to describe, explain or predict outcomes of real or imaginary events.	•Demonstrate Curiosity and ask Questions •Engage in problem solving techniques. •Use words to discuss predictions •Use language to reiterate process and conclusions •Use language to describe objects by a variety of attributes	•Gross Motor: balance and coordination.

Notes: What did your child do well? Are there any skills they need to continue to work on?

A2. Train Car - Activity time: 15 minutes

Materials Needed
☐ One (1) Package of Crayons or Markers
☐ Two (2) Pieces of Plain White Paper cut in half
☐ One (1) Blank Piece of Lined Paper

Instructions:

Step 1: Ask your child to name each room in their home. Write down what they say on a blank piece of lined paper. **For Example**: Kitchen, Bathroom, Living Room, Bedroom… etc.

Step 2: Tell your child that sometimes people ride trains to get from one place to another. On each train, there are different sections called "train cars". Each of these cars has a different purpose.

Step 3: The **first car** is called the **engine**. This is where the driver ("engineer") sits and steers the train.

Step 4: Ask your child to draw a picture of the engine/engineer on one of the half- sheets of blank paper.

Step 5: There are on the train and are used for different purposes. There is a dining car where people eat. There is a sleeper car where people sleep and there is a sitting car where people relax when they're awake.

Step 6: Direct the child to draw a picture of people sleeping on beds on one of the blank pieces of paper. These people are in the **sleeping car** of the train.

Step 7: Direct the child to draw a picture of a people sitting on chairs on one of the blank pieces of paper. These people are in the **Sitting car** of the train.

Step 8: Direct the child to draw a picture of a people eating on one of the blank pieces of paper. These people are in the **eating car** of the train.

Step 9: Let's arrange the pictures in a horizontal line in the following order:

1) Engine   2) sleeper car   3) eating car   4) sitting car.

Step 10: Once the child has arranged the cars, ask them to count how many cars there are (Answer: Four Train Cars.)

Step 11: Ask your child to identify which **space the sleeping car is in**. Is it in the First, Second, Third or Fourth spot? Answer: The sleeper car is the **second** car in that row.

Step 12: Explain to your child that the word **"second"** is called an **"ordinal number"**. Ordinal numbers are **words that explain a position of something**. In this instance, the Sleeper Car is second in the line of train cars.

Step 13: Ask the child to identify which spot the **sitting car** is in, using an **ordinal number**. Can they count each car and tell you the sleeper car is number four?
Answer: The Sitting Car is the **FOURTH** car!

Step 14: Ask your child to rearrange all of the cars and place them in **any order** they would like.

Step 15: Ask your child to use the **ordinal number** when describing which spot the **sleeper car** is in. Do they know?

Step 16: Continue to ask them which spot the rest of the cars are in. Do they know the ordinal number (Ordinal numbers include "first", "second", "third" etc.)?

Step 17: Repeat steps 13 and 14 two more times. Can the child identify spaces that each car is in after each rearrangement?

A.2 Learning Objectives

Math/Science	Language/Literacy	Problem Solving	Motor Skills
•One to one correspondence. •Recognizes the names of Numerals.	•Follow new directions. •Use sentences in conversation to describe, explain or predict outcomes of real or imaginary events. •Build Vocabulary	•Demonstrate Curiosity and ask Questions •Engage in problem solving techniques. •Use words to discuss predictions •Use language to reiterate process and conclusions •Use language to describe objects by a variety of attributes	•Fine Motor: Use a pencil to other writing tool to draw.

Notes: What did your child do well? Are there any skills they need to continue to work on?

A3. Cars and Trucks - Activity time: 20 minutes

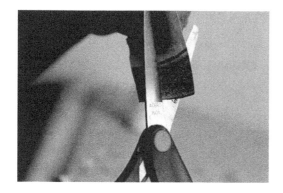

Materials Needed
- ☐ Two (2) or Three (3) Auto Part Magazines or Sale Papers
- ☐ One (1) Pair of child-safe scissors

Instructions

Step 1: Tell your child to look through the magazines or sale papers and use child-safe scissors to cut out **10 pictures of cars** and **10 pictures of trucks**.

Step 2: Encourage your child to sort the vehicles into piles with **2 similar characteristics**.

Examples of **2 characteristics:**

a) Color and Style

b) Size (large or small) and Make/Model

Step 3: Encourage the child to finish to making the following patterns, using the sorted piles of pictures they created:

a) Car, car, truck, car, car, truck….
b) Truck, truck, car, truck, truck, car…
c) Car, truck, car, truck, car, truck…
d) Car, car, truck, truck, truck, car, car, truck, truck, truck….

Step 4: Encourage the child to make new patterns by color, size and type of cars they found.

Step 5: Ask your child about each car and truck in the pattern. What makes characteristics make the cars the same?

A.3 Learning Objectives

Math/Science	Language/Literacy	Problem Solving	Motor Skills
•Count up to 20 objects, using one to one correspondence. •Understands size words (Smaller vs. Larger). •Describe shapes by at least two characteristics. •Complete patterns that have two or more elements. •Sort objects into groups by two or more attributes.	•Follow directions.	•Demonstrate Curiosity and ask Questions •Use language to describe objects by a variety of attributes.	•Fine Motor: Use scissors to cut out an object.

Notes: What did your child do well? Are there any skills they need to continue to work on?

**A4. Unicycles vs. Bicycles vs. Tricycles - **Activity time: All Day

Materials Needed
- ☐ Three (3) white, blank pieces of paper
- ☐ One (1) pen
- ☐ One (1) yellow highlighter
- ☐ Access to the internet

Instructions:

Step 1: Ask the child if they know what a:

- A unicycle looks like?
- A bicycle looks like?
- A tricycle looks like?

Step 2: Explain that unicycles look like bicycles, but they **have only one wheel.** Look at pictures on the Internet of people riding unicycles.

An example of a video or an adult riding a unicycle is:
The ABC of Unicycle Tricks by edononewheel.

You can find the YouTube video here:
https://www.youtube.com/watch?v=2-TRSgdba_g

Step 3: Ask your child to draw a picture of **a unicycle** on a blank piece of white paper. Explain to the child that **"uni" means "one".** How many wheels does the "unicycle" have?

Step 4: The adult should use a yellow highlighter to write the number **"1" inside the wheel** the child drew.

Step 5: Encourage the child to trace the number 1 with a pen.

Step 6: Now ask the child **how many wheels there are on a bicycle.** Explain to them the **"bi" means "two".** There are **two wheels** on a "bicycle."

Step 7: On another sheet of blank paper, ask the child to draw a picture of a bicycle with **two wheels.**

Step 8: When completed, the adult should use a yellow highlighter and **draw a "1" inside one wheel of the bicycle and a "2" inside the other wheel**.

Step 9: Encourage the child to trace the numbers with a pen.

Step 10: Now ask the child **how many wheels a tricycle has**? Tell them that **"tri" means "3"**. There are three wheels on a "**tri**cycle."

Step 11: On the last piece of blank paper, ask the child to draw a picture of a **tricycle** with **three wheels.**

Step 12: When completed, the adult show use a **yellow highlighter draw a "1" inside one of the wheels on the tricycle, a "2" inside of the second wheel and "3" inside of the other wheel.**

Step 13: Encourage the child to trace the numbers with a pen.

Step 14: Place all three of the pictures in front of the child. Ask them to point to the picture that has "3" wheels. Can recognizing the numbers they traced inside the wheels?

Step 15: Ask the child to point to the picture with "1" wheel.

Step 16: Repeat step 15, asking the child to identify the different "cycle" pictures:

- Point to the unicycle.
- Point to the bicycle.
- Point to the tricycle.

Step 17: Practice counting the wheels and recognizing written numbers.

A.4 Learning Objectives

Math/Science	Language/Literacy	Problem Solving	Motor Skills
•Solve simple addition and subtractions problems with objects. •Count using one to one correspondence. •Recognizes the names of Numerals. •Identify objects by two attributes.	•Identify meaning of words based on prefixes	•Demonstrate Curiosity and ask Questions •Engage in problem solving techniques. •Use words to discuss predictions •Use language to reiterate process and conclusions •Use language to describe objects by a variety of attributes.	•Fine Motor: Use a pen or marker to draw. •Fine Motor: Use a pencil to trace new words or numbers

Notes: What did your child do well? Are there any skills they need to continue to work on?

A5. The Gas Station - Activity time: 20 minutes

Materials Needed
- ☐ Twenty (20) index cards (any color)
- ☐ One (1) Blank Sheet of White paper
- ☐ One (1) Black Marker
- ☐ One (1) Yellow Highlighter

Instructions:

Step 1: Explain to the child that today you're going to talk about how to take care of your car. Your car needs to eat also. They don't eat food, but they do use **gasoline, electricity or other types of "fuel"** to work.

Step 2: Today, you're going to find out how much money it will take **to fill up a car's gas tank**.

Step 3: Tell the child that you have a car that **needs 8 gallons of gas to fill** up its gas tank.

Step 4: Today, gas costs **$2 per gallon**.

Step 5: Using the black marker, tell the child to make eight tally mark lines on the piece of blank white paper.

l	l	l	l	l	l	l	l

Step 6: Next, tell the child they **need to have $2 for every tally mark they drew**. That's how we will find out how much money it will cost to put 8 gallons of gas in your car.

Step 7: Explain to the child that each index card represents one dollar ($1).

Step 8: Tell the child to **count two index cards for each tally mark**. Direct them to put two index cards under each of the eight tally marks.

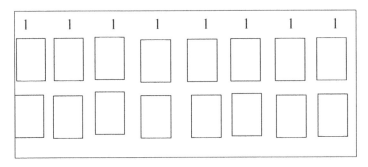

Step 9: Help them add up the total amount of cards to see how much money they need to pay for gas today (16 cards = $16.00).

Step 10: While the child counts each index card, the adult should use a yellow highlighter to write each number on the index card. Write number 1 on the first card, number 2 on the second card… and so on until the adult writes number 16 on the last card. See Example Below:

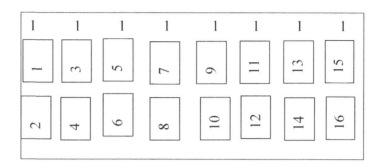

Step 11: This means that it will take **sixteen dollars** to buy the **eight gallons of gas** to fill up their car.

Step 12: Encourage the child to use the black marker to trace the numbers written on the index cards.

Step 13: Tell the child to use the index card (money) in their pretend play area.

A.5 Learning Objectives

Math/Science	Language/Literacy	Problem Solving	Motor Skills
•Solve simple addition and subtractions problems with objects. •Introduction to Multiplication Concepts •Count up to 16 objects, using one to one correspondence. •Recognizes the names of Numerals.	•Follow directions. •Use sentences in conversation to describe, explain or predict outcomes of real or imaginary events.	•Demonstrate Curiosity and ask Questions •Engage in problem solving techniques. •Use words to discuss predictions •Use language to reiterate process and conclusions •Use a variety of techniques to record information and data collection	•Fine Motor: Use a pencil to trace new words or numbers

Notes: What did your child do well? Are there any skills they need to continue to work on?

Language Development – Growing our Vocabulary

By Completing Level 3 Activities, We will learn how to…

- o Follow three-step directions.
- o Use sentences in conversation to describe, explain or predict outcomes of real or imaginary events.
- o Initiate and engage in literacy activities.

Literacy Development – Beginning Reading and Writing

By Completing Level 3 Activities, We will learn how to..

- o Write their own name, without help.
- o Write familiar words by looking at the word then copying.
- o Identify all letters by sight and sound

B1. The Helicopter Ride - Activity time: 15 minutes

Materials Needed
☐ Access to the Internet
☐ Two (2) Blank Sheets of White Paper
☐ One (1) Pen or Marker
☐ One (1) Box of Crayons
☐ One (1) Highlighter

Instructions:

Step 1: Watch a video about a helicopter flying over something. There are many Videos on YouTube. Yhis YouTube video of a helicopter flying over Niagara Falls is spectacular!

Niagara Helicopters Ride, Niagara Falls (full HD)' by Ujjwal Kumar
https://www.youtube.com/watch?v=01ER7l-LrKl

Step 2: Tell the child you are going to write a story about a helicopter ride they would like to go on. Ask the child the following questions and write their responses down:

A) What color helicopter would you like to ride in?

B) How many feet high would you go in the helicopter?

C) What would you like to see when looking down at the ground?

D) If you were to go on a helicopter ride, what do you think would happen?

Step 3: Ask your child to trace the words and numbers the adult wrote down. Can they identify the numbers and the letters and they trace them?

Step 4: Explain to your child that the author is the person who writes a story. They are the author if this story.

Step 5: Ask your child to write their name at the top of the piece of paper. They are the author!

Step 6: Ask your child to come up with a name for this helicopter story.

Step 7: This name is called the Title of the story! Help your child write the Title at the top of the piece of paper.

Step 8: Allow your child to draw a photo that explains their helicopter ride.

Step 9: Attach the story and the photo together and review it later with your child.

Step 10: At a later date, ask your child if they would like to add another chapter to their story. Repeat Steps 2 through 9!

B.1 Learning Objectives

Math/Science	Language/Literacy	Problem Solving	Motor Skills
• Recognizes the names of Numerals. • Understands size words (Smaller vs. Larger).	• Write their own name, without help. • Use sentences in conversation to describe, explain or predict outcomes of real or imaginary events. • Identify all letters by sight and sound	• Demonstrate Curiosity and ask Questions • Engage in problem solving techniques.	• Fine Motor: Use a pen or marker to write familiar words. • Fine Motor: Use a pencil to trace new words and numbers.

Notes: What did your child do well? Are there any skills they need to continue to work on?

B2. The Great Big Car - Activity time: 15 minutes

Materials Needed
- ☐ One (1) large piece of blank paper
- ☐ One (1) pen
- ☐ One (1) package of markers or crayons
- ☐ One (1) blank piece of lined paper

Instructions:

Step 1: It's time to create a story about your family car. Ask your child the following questions and write down what they say on a blank piece of paper:

- What does your car look like?
- Where they went the last time they rode in the car?
- Who rides in the car with you?
- Where is your favorite place to go in the car?

Step 2: Ask your child to trace the words to the answers they gave.

Step 3: Give the child the blank sheet of paper and some crayons or markers. Tell the child to draw a picture of your family car.

Step 4: Ask your child to explain the picture to you. Were they able to recreate your real car using the actual color, amount of wheels, type of car, etc.?

Step 5: Ask your child to write their name on the photo.

Optional: Go to a car sales lot with the child. Can they find other cars that are the same color as your family car? Which cars do they like the best?

B.2 Learning Objectives

Math/Science	Language/Literacy	Problem Solving	Motor Skills
•Recognizes the names of Numerals. •Understands size words (Smaller vs. Larger). •Describe shapes by at least two characteristics.	•Write their own name, without help. •Use sentences in conversation to describe, explain or predict outcomes of real or imaginary events. •Write familiar words by looking at the word then copying. •Identify all letters by sight and sound.	•Use a variety of techniques to record information and data collection •Use language to describe objects by a variety of attributes	•Fine Motor: Use a pen or marker to write familiar words. •Fine Motor: Use a pencil to trace new words

Notes: What did your child do well? Are there any skills they need to continue to work on?

B3. The Little Me That Could - Activity time: 25 minutes

Materials Needed
☐ One (1) Access to the Internet
☐ One (1) Piece of lined paper
☐ One (1) Pen
☐ One (1) Piece of blank, white paper
☐ One (1) Package or markers or crayons
☐ Access to the Internet

Instructions:

Step 1: Read the story The Little Engine that Could by Watty Piper. If you don't have the book or can't make it to the library, you can watch it on the Internet.

One Internet Audio Book of 'The Little Engine that Could', read by Matthew Abeler.
https://www.youtube.com/watch?v=Vd-jgJOP-Ww

Step 2: Ask your child to tell you what happened to the little engine. Why was the engine sad?

Step 3: Ask your child what happened when the little engine said, "I think I can".

Step 4: Ask your child what tasks they have difficulty completing?

(Some common answers: getting dressed by myself, putting a puzzle together, remembering to go to the potty, etc).

Write down what they say on the piece of lined paper with a pen.

Step 5: Have your child repeat the phrase "I think I can, I think I can ___(answers from step 5)___".

Step 6: Ask your child draw a picture of what they can do really well.

Step 7: Ask them what they drew. The adult should write "I did it" underneath the drawing with a black pen or marker.

Step 8: Have your child trace the words "I did it!"

Step 9: Ask your child to write their name at the bottom of their picture.

Step 10: Hang the picture up on the wall and tell the child that if they ever need help, always ask an adult for support.

B.3 Learning Objectives

Math/Science	Language/Literacy	Problem Solving	Motor Skills
•N/A	•Write their own name, without help.	•.Use words to discuss predictions	•Fine Motor: Use a pen or marker to write familiar words.
	•Use sentences in conversation to describe, explain or predict outcomes of real or imaginary events.	•Use language to reiterate process and conclusions.	•Fine Motor: Use a pencil to trace new words
	•Initiate and engage in literacy activities.		
	•Write familiar words by looking at the word then copying.		
	•Identify all letters by sight and sound		

Notes: What did your child do well? Are there any skills they need to continue to work on?

B4. Red, Green and Yellow - Activity time: 15 minutes

Materials Needed
- ☐ One (1) Piece of Red Construction Paper
- ☐ One (1) Piece of Green Construction Paper
- ☐ One (1) Piece of Yellow Construction Paper
- ☐ One (1) Familiar Children's book that your family reads often

Instructions:

Step 1: Tell the child that when you're driving the car, you have to **pay attention** to the stoplights on the road.

Red means 'stop',

Yellow means 'slow down'

Green means 'go'

Step 2: Today you're going to practice following these **"color directions"** while reading a favorite book.

Step 3: Show the child the green, **yellow** and red pieces of construction paper.

Step 4: Tell the child they will be in charge of holding up the colored paper and you will respond by **stopping, slowing down** or starting (go) to **read**. Let them know it will be their turn to "read" (pretend to read or reiterate the story from memory) when you're done.

Step 4: Give the child the three pieces of colored paper. Once you start reading, follow their "paper" directions:

- START to read when they hold up the green paper
- STOP reading when they show you the red paper
- **READ SLOWLY** when they hold up the **yellow paper**

Step 5: Once the adult has finished reading the book, it's time to switch. Allow the child to "read" the book to you. Hold up the green paper to signify for them to start. While they're telling you the story, change up the colored paper to see if they remember to slow down, stop or go!

Step 6: You can repeat this activity multiple times while looking through a variety of books!

B.4 Learning Objectives

Math/Science	Language/Literacy	Problem Solving	Motor Skills
•Describe and identify symbolic meaning. •Show understanding of measurement by using measuring tools (Speed: Fast vs. Slow vs. Stop)	•Use sentences in conversation to describe, explain or predict outcomes of real or imaginary events. •Initiate and engage in literacy activities.	•Demonstrate Curiosity and ask Questions •Engage in problem solving techniques. •Use words to discuss predictions •Use language to reiterate process and conclusions •Use language to describe objects by a variety of attributes •Color Identification	•Fine Motor: Turn Pages of a Book One at a Time.

Notes: What did your child do well? Are there any skills they need to continue to work on?

✎ **B5. My Driven Name -** Activity time: 15 minutes

Materials Needed
- ☐ One (1) small plastic or metal toy car
- ☐ One (1) piece of blank, white paper
- ☐ One (1) black marker
- ☐ One (1) tablespoon of finger paint (any color)
- ☐ One (1) paper plate

Instructions:

Step 1: Write the child's name in large letters on the blank piece of paper. Make sure to use Uppercase and Lowercase Letters.

Step 2: Place one tablespoon of finger paint on a paper plate.

Step 3: Tell the child to dip the wheels of the toy car into the finger paint and drive the car along the lines of their name, written in black marker, tracing their name with the wheels.

Step 4: When completed, hold it up so they can see their Track Name!

Step 5: On another piece of blank paper, write the child's last name in large letters. Encourage the child to repeat step 3, tracing their last name with the car wheels. Can they name each letter?

B.5 Learning Objectives

Math/Science	Language/Literacy	Problem Solving	Motor Skills
•N/A	•Identify all letters by sight and sound •Follow Directions •Name Recognition	•Use language to describe objects by a variety of attributes.	•Fine Motor: Trace words

Notes: What did your child do well? Are there any skills they need to continue to work on?

Gross Motor – Using our large muscles to move!

By Completing Level 3 Activities, We will learn…

- o **Participate in a variety of gross motor activities that require balance and coordination.**
- o **Hop on one foot five or more times.**

Fine Motor – Using our hands to complete tasks

By Completing Level 3 Activities, We will learn…

- o **Use scissors to cut out an object.**
- o **Use a pen or marker to write familiar words.**
- o **Use a pencil to trace new words.**

C1. Wheel Rolling - Activity time: 15 minutes

Materials Needed
- ☐ Four (4) Different sized, round balls (Basketball, Soccer Ball, Tennis Ball, Ping Pong Ball, Golf Ball, etc)
- ☐ One (1) Stick of Sidewalk Chalk

Instructions:

Step 1: Use sidewalk chalk to draw two 12-inch lines, four feet apart from each other, on the sidewalk.

Step 2: Ask the child to line all of the balls up on one 12-inch line.

Step 3: All of the balls are going to represent wheels, because they are round. Using either the child's left or right foot, encourage the child to kick each ball towards the other chalk line (drawn four feet away).

Step 4: Ask the child to child count how many kicks it takes for each ball to get across the other line. Using the sidewalk chalk, write down the number of kicks.

Step 5: Which ball took the least amounts of kicks?

Step 6: Repeat step 3 and 4 as long as they would like.

Step 7: Ask the child to look at the numbers written in chalk. Can they identify which number is that largest? Which number is the smallest?

Optional: Draw a set of two more lines with a larger distance between the lines. Repeat Steps 2 through 6.

C.1 Learning Objectives

Math/Science	Language/Literacy	Problem Solving	Motor Skills
•Solve simple addition subtractions problems with objects. •One to one correspondence. •Recognizes the names of Numerals. •Sort objects by two attributes. •Show understanding of measurement by using measuring tools.	•Follow directions. •Use sentences in conversation.	•Demonstrate Curiosity and ask Questions •Use language to reiterate process and conclusions •Use a variety of techniques to record information and data collection •Use language to describe objects by a variety of attributes	•Gross Motor: balance and coordination.

Notes: What did your child do well? Are there any skills they need to continue to work on?

C2. Practice Rides - Activity time: 15 minutes

Materials Needed
☐ One (1) Child's bike (This can be whatever the child is currently using: tricycle, bike with training wheels, child-sized bike, etc).
☐ One (1) Stick of Sidewalk Chalk

Instructions:

Step 1: Using the sidewalk chalk, draw a long "track" on the sidewalk. It should include different directions; up and down, to the left and right, and go around in circles. Make sure the track follows a safe area on a sidewalk or pavement where the child can ride his/her bike. **Try to make the track at least fifteen feet long.**

Step 2: Tell the child it's their turn to ride their bike on the track. Make sure they follow the track like it's a road, making all the turns along the way.

Step 3: Ask your child to tell you the direction they are turning turns. Example: I'm turning right.

C.2 Learning Objectives

Math/Science	Language/Literacy	Problem Solving	Motor Skills
•N/A	•Follow directions. •Use sentences in conversation to describe, explain or predict outcomes of real or imaginary events.	•Use words to discuss predictions •Use language to reiterate process and conclusions	•Gross Motor: balance and coordination.

Notes: What did your child do well? Are there any skills they need to continue to work on?

C3. My Own Two Feet - Activity time: 15 minutes

Materials Needed
☐ A large outdoor space that has room for running.

Instructions:

Step 1: Tell the child that some people aren't able to ride in cars, busses or airplanes. Instead, they use their feet to get to different places. If they don't have bicycles, skateboards or other modes of transportation, people can **walk and run**.

Step 2: Take the child to a safe, outdoor area where they're able to run. Pick a spot where your child will start their run.

Step 3: The adult should walk at least 50 steps away from where the child is standing. This will be the "finish" line.

Step 4: Tell the child you're going to start counting to see how long it will take them to get from the starting point (where they are standing) to the finish line (where the adult is).

Step 5: On your mark, get set, go!!! Start counting! How long does it take for the child to get to the finish line? Our feet can move us fast when we need to get somewhere.

Step 6: Ask your child to repeat the activity.

Step 7: Tell your child the two numbers:

- How long did it take for them to get to the finish line the first time?
  Example: Counted to 15

- How long did it take for them to get the finish line the second time?
  Example: Counted to 12

Step 8: Ask your child which time they got there the quickest? Which number is the smallest?

Step 6: Repeat as many times as you would like!

C.3 Learning Objectives

Math/Science	Language/Literacy	Problem Solving	Motor Skills
• Count up to 20 objects, using one to one correspondence. • Recognizes the names of Numerals. • Understands size words (Smaller vs. Larger).	• Use sentences in conversation to describe, explain or predict outcomes of real or imaginary events.	• Use words to discuss predictions • Use language to reiterate process and conclusions	• Gross Motor: balance and coordination.

Notes: What did your child do well? Are there any skills they need to continue to work on?

C4. Galloping - Activity time: 20 minutes

Materials Needed
☐ Access to the Internet.
☐ One (1) Pen
☐ One (1) Yellow Highlighter
☐ One (1) Piece of scotch tape
☐ Access to outdoor space

Instructions:

Step 1: Take the child to a place where adults and children horseback ride. If that isn't possible, watch a video on the Internet of horseback riding. One example of a YouTube video of people horseback riding is: <u>Horseback Riding in Hawaii</u> by Annie Huber.

Step 2: Tell the child that horses **gallop** because they have **four legs**. When they move all of their feet are off of the ground at the same time.

Step 3: Next, tell the child that it's their turn to pretend to gallop like a horse.

Step 4: The adult should use a yellow highlighter to write the word "Horse" on a blank piece of paper.

Step 5: Tell the child to trace the yellow letters with a pen.

Step 6: Tape the "horse" sign to the back of the child's shirt and tell them they are now a galloping horse!

Step 7: Encourage them to gallop around the outdoors (in a safe area), just like a horse!

C.4 Learning Objectives

Math/Science	Language/Literacy	Problem Solving	Motor Skills
•N/A	•Write familiar words by looking at the word then copying. •Identify all letters by sight and sound	•Engage in problem solving techniques. •Use language to reiterate process and conclusions. •Demonstrate understanding of differences between people, animals, plants and other parts of the planet	•Gross Motor: balance and coordination. •Fine Motor: Use a pen or marker to write familiar words. •Fine Motor: Use a pencil to trace new words

Notes: What did your child do well? Are there any skills they need to continue to work on?

C5. Tire Jump - Activity time: 15 minutes

Materials Needed
- ☐ Five (5) Hula Hoops (Or one piece of sidewalk chalk)
- ☐ An outdoor area

Instructions:

Step 1: Tires are large, round circles that are put on cars, airplanes, trains, bikes and other vehicles. These hula-hoops are large and round just like the tires.

*Note: If you don't have hula hoops, sidewalk chalk can be used.

Step 2: Tell your child to lay the hula-hoops on the ground in any order that they would like. If you are using sidewalk chalk, ask your child to draw 5 large circles on the ground.

Step 3: Now, jump from one hula-hoop (or circle) to another. Continue jumping until they jump in and out of each one.

Step 4: Have them count how many jumps they make (1 jump, 2 jumps, 3 jumps, etc..)

Step 5: Repeat, asking your child to jump on one foot only!

C.5 Learning Objectives

Math/Science	Language/Literacy	Problem Solving	Motor Skills
•Count using one to one correspondence. •Describe shapes.	•N/A	•Demonstrate Curiosity and ask Questions	•Gross Motor: balance and coordination. •Gross Motor: Hop on one foot five or more times.

Notes: What did your child do well? Are there any skills they need to continue to work on?

Themed Project – Package Delivery Systems

Purpose: To teach the process of finding answers to new questions. Each project guides adults and children through investigating specific questions about the theme. The project starts with the development of a hypothesis that is then tested and researched, concluding with an answer to the hypothesis. Specific Learning Objectives include:

> **Problem Solving Skills: By Completing Level 3, We will learn…**
>
> - Predict the results of a familiar action.
> - Develop strategies to solve a problem.
> - Communicate memories about a sequence of related events that happened in the past.
> - Put materials or objects together in new and inventive ways.
> - Participate in challenging multi-step activities/projects
> - Demonstrate Curiosity and ask Questions.
> - Use words to discuss predictions.
> - Use language to reiterate process and conclusions.
> - Use a variety of techniques to record information and data collection.

Includes: Activities and discussions that address all areas of academic and developmental skills that meets the Level 3 Learning Objectives. Includes math, science, literacy, art, health/safety, gross motor skills, fine motor skills, music and movement and literacy development.

Order of Operation: These projects are designed to be followed in the order they are laid out, each activity building on the knowledge acquired from previous activities.

> **Project Objective:** When this project is completed, your child should be able to answer the question:
>
> ### What are the different ways to send mail to people?
>
> This project provides opportunities for child to investigate the different ways packages get from their starting point to their destination. These include air (planes), sea (boats) and land (trucks and trains).

Introduction

Activity #1: How do people and items get to different places?

Step 1: Ask the child if they know the different ways that packages are delivered across the world. Write down exactly what they say on a separate piece of paper. Make sure to keep this piece of paper on hand to revisit when the project is completed.

Step 2: Tell the child there are two different names for packages that are sent across the world.

Step 3: One is called "freight". Freight is when items are placed on a train, car or truck when they are moved.

Step 4: The other name is "cargo". Cargo is when the objects are placed on an airplane or a ship.

Step 5: Tell your child that there is also a third type of "package". It's people! The name for vehicles that carry people are called "passenger."

Step 6: Ask your child to draw a picture of every way that mail/packages/people can travel!

Investigation

Section 1: Where does our mail/packages get to their destination?

A. Air - Cargo Plane

Activity #2:

Materials Needed:
- One (1) Piece of Paper
- One (1) Package of Markers

Instructions

Step 1: Ask the child the following question: Why would someone put a package on an airplane?

Step 2: Listen to what they have to say.

Step 3: Tell them that when a package must travel a long distance, like over an ocean, into another state or to another country it may go on an airplane. Airplanes are able to fly fast so the packages that need to get somewhere quickly are placed on the airplane.

Step 4: When delivering packages across the world, there are many options on how to get the package to its destination. Packages placed on an airplane need to be delivered quickly.

Step 5: Have the child draw a picture of a very important item they would place on an airplane to get somewhere quickly. What are they drawing? Ask them whom they are sending the package to.

B. Truck: Freight

Activity #3:

Materials Needed:
- One (1) Blank Piece of Paper
- One (1) Box of Crayons
- One (1) Sale Paper ads from a grocery store
- One (1) Pair of Child-safe scissors
- One (1) Glue Stick

Instructions:

Step 1: Tell the child that large Semi-Trucks are full of freight. Have they seen one of these when they are traveling down the road? If so, what did it look like?

Step 2: Grocery stores have their own Trucks. Encourage the child to draw a picture of a Semi-Truck that is going to the grocery store filled with their favorite foods.

Step 3: Ask the child to use the child-safe scissors to cut their favorite foods out of the sale paper ads.

Step 4: Ask the child to use the glue stick to glue the food pictures onto the picture of the semi-truck.

Step 5: Ask the child what food they put into their truck. Write down what they say on the bottom of the paper.

C. Ocean Cargo Shipments

Activity #4:

Materials Needed
- One (1) Piece of Paper
- One (1) Box of Markers or Crayons
- One (1) Empty Water Bottle with Lid
- Once (1) Bathtub or small plastic tub filled with water.

Instructions:

Step 1: Tell the child that when packages have to go over an ocean, sometimes the "cargo" is placed on ships. They're called "cargo ships". The packages are carried on the inside of the ship and on the decks (outside of the ship).

Step 2: Ask the child to draw a picture of something they would send to somebody on the other side of an ocean. Would they put their cargo on the **inside** of the ship or **on the deck** of the ship?

Step 3: Tell them to roll up the picture of the item and place it inside the empty water bottle. Make sure to put the cap on.

Step 4: Put the water bottle into a tub of water. It floats! This is a pretend ship with their cargo inside.

Step 5: Ask your child: "Where's it going?"

Step 6: Ask your child to tell you a story about the note. Who it is going to?

Step 7: Ask your child to tell you a story about the trip the note is going to take to get there.

D. Freight Trains

Activity #5:

Materials Needed:
- One (1) Blank Piece of Paper
- One (1) Yellow Highlighter
- One (1) Pencil
- One (1) Box of Crayons
- One (1) Glue Stick

Instructions:

Step 1: Ask the child:

- Have you seen a train before?
- What's in all of those train cars?

Step 2: Tell them there are different types of trains - some are for passengers and some are for freight. **Freight means that there are objects on the train, not people**.

Step 4: Ask your child what type of **freight** they would want to put on a train. They can list as many different items as they would like. Write down what they say with a yellow highlighter.

Step 5: Tell the child to use a pencil to trace the words the adult wrote in yellow highlighter, sounding out each letter that they trace.

Step 6: Ask the child to count how many items are on the list (in yellow highlighter).

Step 7: Using a crayon and a blank piece of paper, tell the child to draw a train with the **same amount of freight cars as words they traced in step 6**.

Step 8: When the child is done, have them draw one object they named in Step 6, on each of the train cars that they drew.

Step 9: Ask the child where the train is going and who is going to use the items in the train.

Section 2: How do people get to where they need to go?

Tell the child that people also use a variety of transportation vehicles to arrive at different places. People are able to go on planes, boats and trains too. These are called passenger planes, passenger boats and passenger trains.

Activity #6: Over the Deep Blue Ocean - Activity time: 20 minutes

Materials Needed:

- Access to the Internet
- One (1) set of Crayons
- One (1) pen or pencil
- One (1) Yellow Highlighter

Instructions:

Step 1: Ask the child if they know how boats float? Some people **use boats to get to work**. These boats are called **Ferry Boats**. You can drive your car onto the boat, and the boat will take you and your car to the land on the other side of the water.

Step 2: Encourage the child to draw a picture of a boat using the crayons and the blank piece of white paper.

Step 3: Ask them where the cars go in their boat? Where would the people go in their boat?

Step 4: Now it's time to watch a video of a Ferry Boat to see how cars and people ride on a boat.

Step 5: Watch cars load and unload onto a Ferry Boat on the Internet.

An example of a video is:

'Loading Onto the Ferry Boat' by 1963impala2dr
https://www.youtube.com/watch?v=QeaEN8xPtzQ

Step 6: Ask the child where they think the people on the boat are going to go?

Activity #7: Colorful Cars - Activity time: 30 minutes

Materials Needed
- One (1) Piece of blank Paper
- One (1) Pen
- One (1) Neighborhood safe for walking around with adult.

Instructions:

Step 1: Tell the child you are going to go on a color hunt. You're going to find out what the most popular **car color** is on your block.

Step 2: Take a blank piece of paper and a pen on the walk with you.

Step 3: Tell the child to look at all of the cars you pass while on your walk. When they see one, have them tell you what color it is.

Step 4: When the child tells you a color, write that color down on the piece of paper. Next to the name of the color, draw a tally mark representing the car. If you see more cars of the same color, continue to write a tally mark next to the color.

Step 5: Once you have walked around the neighborhood block, return back to your home to find out which car color is the most popular.

Step 6: Ask the child count the number of tally marks next to each color. Write down the total number of each car color next to the color name.

Example:

> Blue. 1 1 1 **3 blue cars**
> Red. 1 1 **2 red cars**
> Green. 1 **1 green car**
> Brown. 1 **1 brown car**
> Black 1 1 1 1 1 **5 black cars**

Step 7: Ask the child:

- Which car color they saw the most. Which number is the highest?
- Which color did they see the least of? Which number is the lowest?

Activity #8: Airplane Flight - Activity time: 15 minutes

Materials Needed
- Two (2) Pieces of Blank, White construction paper
- Access to the internet
- One (1) Ruler
- One (1) package of markers or crayons
- Two (2) paperclips
- One (1) stick of sidewalk chalk

Instructions:

Step 1: Tell the child that together, you're going to make two paper airplanes.

Step 2: Using the markers or crayons, have the child decorate one piece of paper. The adult should decorate the other.

Step 3: Once you have finished decorating your pieces of paper, look for a "how to create q paper airplane" video on the Internet. One example of is the YouTube video:

 How to Make a Paper Airplane by Howcast.
https://www.youtube.com/watch?v=I0a0p8ygfQM&spfreload=1

Step 4: After you have made the airplanes, find a safe place outdoors to test how far your airplanes will fly. Ready, set, go!!!

Step 5: With a piece of sidewalk chalk, mark where the front of the airplane lands on the sidewalk.

Step 6: Continue flying the airplanes for as long as you like. Whose airplane can go the farthest?

Activity #9: Non-motorized Transportation - Activity time: 20 minutes

Materials Needed
- One (1) Piece of Blank, White Paper
- One (1) Black marker
- One (1) Ruler
- One (1) Box of markers or crayons

Instructions:

Step 1: Fold the piece of paper in half, and then fold it in half again.

Step 2: Open up the paper. There should be four sections separated by fold lines.

Step 3: Trace the fold lines with a black marker.

Step 4: Write one of the following words in each area (See Picture Below):

1) Bike
2) Skateboard
3) Walking
4) Roller Blades

Bike	Skateboard
Walking	Rollers Blades

Step 5: Watch a video of people skateboarding and rollerblading. One example is theYouTube Video:

Skateboarders vs. Rollerbladers by Skate House Media
https://www.youtube.com/watch?v=mNzHCfFs9qA

While watching the video, have the child point to the skateboards and rollerblades. Ask your child the following questions:
- Why are they different?
- What safety gear the people are wearing (helmets, knee pads, wrist guards, goggles, etc)?

Step 6: Give the child the sheet of paper and the box of crayons or markers.

Step 7: Point to the section on the sheet of paper that says 'skateboard'. Ask them what a skateboard looks like. Encourage them to draw a picture of a skateboard in that section.

Step 8: Repeat Step 7 directing the questions to the rest of the three sections (bike, walking, roller blades).

Step 9: When completed, ask the child which modes of 'transportation' they have used before?

Section 3: Conclusion

Activity #10: Identification - Activity time: 20 minutes

Materials Needed
- Access to the Internet

Instructions:

Step 1: Tell the child they're going to guess what type of vehicle they hear when they watch the following YouTube video:

Cars, Trucks and Transportation sounds for Kinds-learn-school-preschool-kindergarten : by Annie Sullivan.
https://www.youtube.com/watch?v=4X0pp9MF68s&list=PLpr7IU-v-HzA5_i-zlyYcrumwq1XBymj6

Step 2: Can the child guess what type of transportation vehicle makes each sound?

Step 3: When the curtain opens, ask the child to identify **three different aspects** of each vehicle.
For example:

    A) The Bike – Has two wheels. The wheels are circles. It has a red seat.
    B) The Train – It is green. It has yellow windows. It is driving on tracks.
    C) The Car – It is green. It has one door. It has two wheels.
    D) Etc....

Step 4: When the video is over, ask the child which vehicle was their favorite.

Step 5: After you're finished with this project, ask the child if they want to know anything else about transportation. You may be surprised about their answers! Write them down and encourage them to use books and videos to find out the answers to their questions.

....

Thanks for playing! See you in the next Unit
Pre-K My Way - Level 3, Unit 3
Discovering Weather

JDEducational
Play · Learn · Grow

Pre-K YOUR Way

Level 3 Unit 3

Weather
Discovering the Elements Project

Weather Themed Items For Indoor Learning Environment

Now that you have set up your environment, you are ready to place materials in it that directly relate to the theme you are studying! Here are some suggestions of materials your child can free-play with during the "Exploring My Community" Theme:

Books: Age-appropriate books that directly correlate with the monthly theme can be found at your local library or bought separately online. This is a great opportunity to take a trip with your child to your local library and go on a search together. Have them identify words or pictures on the cover of children's books that correlate to the theme. Place a variety of books related to the theme in your child's book area. This will increase opportunities for them to expand their knowledge and use what they learn in the activities to comprehend what they read in the books.

These are age-appropriate books that directly correlate with the monthly theme, which can be found at your local library or bought separately online.

Weather Themed Items for Indoor Learning Environment

Books

These are age-appropriate books that directly correlate with the monthly theme, which can be found at your local library or bought separately online.

Weather Words and What They Mean – by Gail Gibbons

Like a Windy Day – by Frank Asch and Devin Asch

What's the Weather Like Today – by Conrad J. Storad

Elmo and Abby's Wacky Weather Day – by John Weidman

Stormy Weather– by Debi Gliori

It Looked Like Spilt Milk – by Charles G. Shaw

Cloudy With a Chance of Meatballs – by Judi Barrett and Isidre Mones

Art Area: Encourage your child use this throughout each day by rotating items in an art area. These can be items have already been painted on, paper that they drew on already or leftover materials from another project. Thought provoking art projects are created when children are given unlimited opportunities to explore a variety of materials.

Some suggestions for the art area include:
- Crayons
- Paper
- Pens
- Empty Boxes (all kinds)
- Empty Toilet Paper or Paper Towel Rolls
- Foil
- Clean Q-tips for painting
- Scraps of paper
- Scraps of Yarn
- Scraps of any type of material – including fabric, sand paper, etc.
- Paper Bags
- Straws
- Popsicle Sticks
- Anything else that can be reused.

Suggested Cooking Activities

These are simple cooking and snack-time activities that correlate with the theme. The children can prepare these snacks with adult assistance.

1. **My Cloudy Cracker** – Allow the child to put cream cheese (cloud) onto a cracker. Can they make shapes in the cream cheese using a toothpick?

2. **My Little Snowman -** Attach two marshmallows together using one toothpick. Allow the child to decorate the snowmen. Use frosting as "glue" to attach small candies as the eyes, nose and mouth. Allow the child to use small pretzels for the arms and an Oreo cookie for the hat.

Sensory Bin Suggestions

A sensory bin is a small plastic bucket that is filled with a variety of materials. Sensory bins provide a space to engage in sensory-rich activities that offer opportunities to investigate textures while providing activities for relaxation and self-regulation. Sensory bins encourage language development, small motor development and control, spatial concepts, problem-solving skills and scientific observations. Each month there are suggested sensory bin materials that correlate with the theme of the unit.

Set Up Instructions: In a Plastic Bucket, rotate the following sensory activities throughout the month.

1. **Sand Writing Table:**

    Mix 2 cups of sand, 1 ½ cups cold water and 1 cup of cornstarch together. Stir the mixture for five to ten minutes over medium heat until it becomes thick. Pour the thick sand onto a cookie sheet. After it cools, have your child practice writing the Letter of the Week, Number of the Week and drawing the Shape of the Week in the sand.
    Note: You can also use this mixture to build sand castles that will stick together longer.

2. **Water investigation:**

    Add the following items to the water bin: water, eyedroppers, funnels, cups, spoons, magnifying glasses, rocks and sea animals. Allow the child to play and investigate with these materials.

3. **Rainbow Ice Melting:**

    Freeze a large block of ice in the freezer by filling up an empty cardboard milk carton with water and placing it in the freezer. Once frozen, cut the block of ice out of the carton. Place the ice in a sensory bin. Fill up some plastic cups with a mixture of one cup of water and one tablespoon of salt. Add two food-coloring drops to each cup. Have the child use an eyedropper to suck up the salt water and put it on the frozen block of ice. It melts!!

Dramatic Play Area

This play area allows children to understand and experience the adult world through imitation and creativity. The dramatic play area provides a safe space for young children to create stories while practicing new vocabulary and practicing social skills. It is also a space where groups of children engage in pretend play which provides opportunities to learn self-help skills, share space and materials, take turns and the use abstract thinking. Each month there is a list of suggested materials to integrate into this area, which correlate with the theme of the month.

Suggested props to include in the dramatic play/pretend play area include:

- Small Pop-up tent
- Sandals/flip flops
- Boots
- Socks
- Mittens/Gloves
- Hats
- Sunglasses
- Rain jacket/Snow Jacket
- Scarves
- Umbrella

Learning Objectives - Level 3

After completing all modules in the Level 3 Curriculum Series, the child should be able to:

Mathematics
- Solve simple addition and subtractions problems with objects.
- Count up to 20 objects, using one to one correspondence.
- Recognizes the names of Numerals.
- Understands size words (Smaller vs. Larger).
- Describe shapes by at least two characteristics.
- Complete patterns that have two or more elements.
- Sort objects into groups by two or more attributes.
- Show understanding of measurement by using measuring tools.

Science
- Demonstrate Curiosity and ask Questions
- Engage in problem solving techniques.
- Use words to discuss predictions
- Use language to reiterate process and conclusions
- Use a variety of techniques to record information and data collection
- Use language to describe objects by a variety of attributes
- Demonstrate understanding of differences between people, animals, plants and other parts of the planet.
- Complete multi-step projects.

Language and Literacy
- Write their own name, without help.
- Follow three-step directions.
- Use sentences in conversation to describe, explain or predict outcomes of real or imaginary events.
- Initiate and engage in literacy activities.
- Write familiar words by looking at the word then copying.
- Identify all letters by sight and sound

Problem Solving Skills
- Predict the results of a familiar action.
- Develop strategies to solve a problem.
- Communicate memories about a sequence of related events that happened in the past.
- Put materials or objects together in new and inventive ways.
- Participate in challenging multi-step activities.

Gross Motor/Fine Motor Development
- Participate in a variety of gross motor activities that require balance and coordination.
- Hop on one foot five or more times.
- Use scissors to cut out an object.
- Use a pen or marker to write familiar words.
- Use a pencil to trace new words

Part 1: Weather Themed Academic Activities

These activities have been developed to meet specific, age-appropriate, Kindergarten-Readiness skills. These skills are specified in the learning objectives of each activity. The following activities may be completed in any order desired and are specifically designed to address the academic domains: math, science, language, literacy, cognitive, problem solving, and physical development.

Each activity is on its own page. If the adult chooses to print the activities, the space below each activity is provided for adults to write notes regarding the activity. Adults are encouraged to note if the child enjoyed the activity and if the child needs to work on specific learning objectives. Each activity can be repeated more than once to enable the child to master the learning objectives designed for that activity.

A. Math/Science Development

1. Counting Raindrops
2. Ice Cube Dunk
3. Sock Sort
4. Weather Watch
5. Shoe Classification

B. Language/Literacy Development

1. Sound Game
2. Hot ABCs
3. The Very Cold Day
4. Wet Words
5. Snowy Name

C. Physical Development - Gross Motor & Fine-Motor

1. Puddle Jump
2. Spray Bottle Tag
3. Shapely Sun
4. Thunder Rolls
5. Lightening Balance

Mathematical Development – Understanding Numbers and their Purpose

By Completing Level 3 Activities, We will learn how to...

- o Solve simple addition and subtractions problems with objects.
- o Count up to 20 objects, using one to one correspondence.
- o Recognizes the names of Numerals.
- o Understands size words (Smaller vs. Larger).
- o Describe shapes by at least two characteristics.
- o Complete patterns that have two or more elements.
- o Sort objects into groups by two or more attributes.
- o Show understanding of measurement by using measuring tools.

Science/Cognitive Development – Learning How to Solve Problems

By Completing Level 3 Activities, We will learn how to..

- o Demonstrate Curiosity and ask Questions
- o Engage in problem solving techniques.
- o Use words to discuss predictions
- o Use language to reiterate process and conclusions
- o Use a variety of techniques to record information and data collection
- o Use language to describe objects by a variety of attributes
- o Demonstrate understanding of differences between people, animals, plants and other parts of the planet.
- o Complete multi-step projects.

A1. Counting Raindrops - Activity time: 15 minutes

Materials Needed
- ☐ One (1) Piece of Blank, White Paper.
- ☐ One (1) Black Marker.
- ☐ One (1) Yellow Highlighter
- ☐ One (1) Set of watercolor paints with small paintbrush.
- ☐ One (1) Small, plastic cup filled with water.

Instructions:

Step 1: Use a black marker to draw **10 large circles** on a piece of blank paper. These circles represent clouds.

Step 2: Tell the child to dip the paintbrush into the blue watercolor paint.

Step 3: Direct the child to put **one** drop of blue watercolor paint **into the middle** of each of the circles. These drops represent raindrops.

Step 4: Ask the child to count the total amount of circles (clouds). There are 10 clouds.

Step 5: Ask the child to count the total number of dots (raindrops). There are 10 raindrops. Encourage the child to point to each dot while counting.

Step 5: The adult should use a yellow highlighter to write the numbers that the child says, underneath each of the circles (1 through 10).

Step 6: Ask the child to trace each number with a pen, pencil or marker of their choice, while saying the name of each number.

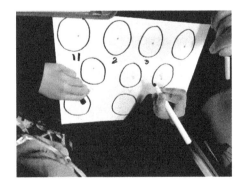

A.1 Learning Objectives

Math/Science	Language/Literacy	Problem Solving	Motor Skills
•Solve simple addition and subtractions problems with objects. •Count up to 10 objects, using one to one correspondence. •Recognizes the names of Numerals.	•.Follow directions. •Use sentences in conversation.	•Use language to reiterate process and conclusions •Use language to describe objects by a variety of attributes.	•Fine Motor: Use a pencil to trace new words or numbers.

Notes: What did your child do well? Are there any skills they need to continue to work on?

A2. Ice Cube Dunk - Activity time: 15 minutes

Materials Needed
- ☐ One (1) Ice Cube Tray full of ice
- ☐ One (1) Pitcher filled with cold water
- ☐ One (1) Small Measuring Cup
- ☐ One (1) Clean Dish Towel

Instructions:

Step 1: The adult should fill a pitcher with cold water and place it on a table.

Step 2: Place **10 ice cubes** onto a kitchen towel next to the water that's on the table.

Step 3: Encourage the child to count each ice cube, pointing to each one while they count.

Step 4: Direct the child to put one ice cube into the pitcher of water.

Step 5: Tell the child to count how many icc cubes are left on the kitchen towel. Have them repeat the phrase:

"(**Ten**) ice cubes minus (take away) **one** makes **(nine)** ice cubes."

Step 6: Repeat steps 3, 4 and 5 until all ice cubes are in the pitcher of cold water.

Step 7: Now ask the child to hold the handle of the measuring cup and scoop **one ice cube out** of the pitcher of cold water, placing the ice cubes back on the clean dishtowel.

Step 8: Direct the child to point to the ice cube and say "one ice cube".

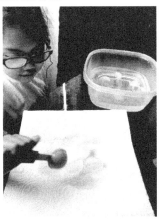

Step 9: Tell the child to scoop out another ice cube and place it on the clean towel, repeating the phrase:

"**One** plus **one** is **two** ice cubes."

Step 10: Repeat steps 7, 8 and 9 until all ice cubes back on the clean towel.

Step 11: Now it's time to drink the ice water!

A.2 Learning Objectives

Math/Science	Language/Literacy	Problem Solving	Motor Skills
•Solve simple addition and subtractions problems with objects. •Count up to 10 objects, using one to one correspondence.	•Use sentences in conversation to describe, explain or predict outcomes of real or imaginary events.	•Engage in problem solving techniques. •Use language to reiterate process and conclusions	•N/A

Notes: What did your child do well? Are there any skills they need to continue to work on?

A3. Sock Sort - Activity time: 20 minutes

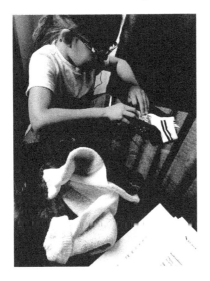

Materials Needed
- ☐ Three (3) Pairs of Adult-sized black socks
- ☐ Three (3) Pairs of Adult-sized white socks
- ☐ Three (3) Pairs of Child-sized black socks
- ☐ Three (3) Pairs of Child-sized white socks

Instructions:

Note – before this activity, separate all the pairs of socks and mix them together in a bucket or an empty bag.

Step 1: Tell the child that when it's cold, you dress warm. To keep our feet warm, we wear socks. You just found a bunch of socks, but they're all mixed up and you need help matching them together.

Step 2: Empty the bag of mixed-up socks into a pile.

Step 3: The adult should find one adult-sized **white sock**, one adult-sized **black sock**, one child-sized **white sock** and one child-sized **black sock.**

Step 4: Place each of the socks from step 3 in a line.

Step 5: The adult should point to each sock (from Step 4) and say the corresponding description (make sure to emphasize the difference between big and small):

- one big black sock
- one big white sock
- one small white sock
- one small black sock.

Step 6: Ask the child to find the matching sock from the sock pile.

Step 7: Each time the child picks up a sock, ask them what **size** and what **color** that sock is.

Step 8: Watch to see if the child can sort the socks by both attributes (**size and color**):

    Example: Attribute 1 = Big; Attribute 2 = Black sock

Step 9: Ask the child to point to the socks that would best fit him/her. Can they put them on by themselves?

Step 10: Ask the child which socks would best fit the adult.

Optional: This activity can be repeated with multiple different colors, patterns and sizes of socks.

A.3 Learning Objectives

Math/Science	Language/Literacy	Problem Solving	Motor Skills
•Count with one to one correspondence. •.Understands size words (Smaller vs. Larger). •Describe shapes by at least two characteristics. •Sort objects into groups by two or more attributes.	•Follow directions.	•Engage in problem solving techniques. •Use language to reiterate process and conclusions •Use language to describe objects by a variety of attributes	•N/A

Notes: What did your child do well? Are there any skills they need to continue to work on?

A4. Weather Watch - Activity time: All Day

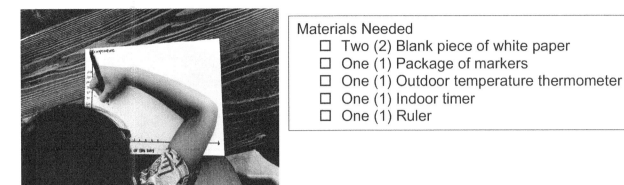

Materials Needed
- ☐ Two (2) Blank piece of white paper
- ☐ One (1) Package of markers
- ☐ One (1) Outdoor temperature thermometer
- ☐ One (1) Indoor timer
- ☐ One (1) Ruler

Instructions:

Step 1: After your child wakes up in the morning, show them an outdoor thermometer. This thermometer tells us how **hot** or **cold** it is outside.

Step 2: Walk outside with your child and place the thermometer in the sun. Once the thermometer has registered the temperature, count the numbers to see what the temperature is outside.

Step 3: Write down the temperature on one piece of paper.

Step 4: Using a ruler, the adult should draw one horizontal line and one vertical line, joining together, to form a graph (see picture below).

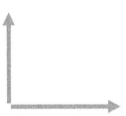

Step 5: Using the ruler make a horizontal mark at each half-inch interval from 0 to 12 inches on the vertical line. Each half-inch space represents ten degrees.

Step 6: Using the ruler mark a horizontal mark at each half-inch interval from 0 to 12 inches on the horizontal line. Each half-inch space represents hours in the day.

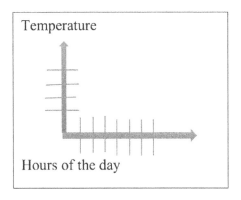

Step 7: Make a dot in the graph for how high or low the temperature was when you measured it.

Step 8: Now, set an indoor timer to two hours.

Step 9: When the timer beeps, repeat step 2 and step 3.

Step 10: Repeat step 7 and step 8.

Step 11: Continue repeating step 9 and step 10 until it is time for bed.

Step 12: Look at the dots that you drew throughout the day with the child. Use a pencil to connect each dot.

Step 13: Discuss how the temperature fluctuates during the day. Discuss how the sun makes the temperature hotter and when the sun goes down, the temperature gets cooler.

A.4 Learning Objectives

Math/Science	Language/Literacy	Problem Solving	Motor Skills
•Count one to one correspondence. •Recognizes the names of Numerals. •Sort objects into groups by two or more attributes. •Show understanding of measurement by using measuring tools.	•Follow directions. •Use sentences in conversation to describe, explain or predict outcomes of real or imaginary events.	•Demonstrate Curiosity and ask Questions •Use words to discuss predictions •Use language to reiterate process and conclusions •Use a variety of techniques to record information and data collection •Use language to describe objects by a variety of attributes	•N/A

Notes: What did your child do well? Are there any skills they need to continue to work on?

A5. Shoe Classification - Activity time: 20 minutes

Materials Needed
- ☐ Two (2) pairs of boots
- ☐ Two (2) pairs of sandals
- ☐ Two (2) pairs of tennis shoes

Instructions:

Step 1: Set all the shoes on the floor. Tell your child that we use different kinds of shoes for different times of the year. Ask them to tell you when they would wear each shoe.
(Example: I wear sandals in the summer and boots in the winter.)

Step 2: The adults should place one sandal, one boot and one tennis shoe in a horizontal line.

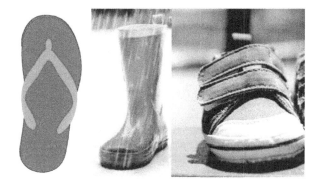

Step 3: Ask the child to point to and name each type of shoe (sandal, boot, tennis shoe).

Step 4: Ask the child to complete the pattern using the rest of the shoes. Can they repeat the pattern three? (Sandal, Boot, Tennis Shoe, Sandal, Boot, Tennis Shoe).

Step 5: Make more patterns together. For example:

- G. Boot, boot, sandal, tennis shoe, boot, boot, sandal, tennis shoe…
- H. Sandal, tennis shoe, tennis shoe, boot, sandal, tennis shoe, tennis shoe, boot…
- I. Add some different types of shoes to the pile and see how many patterns you can create.

A.5 Learning Objectives

Math/Science	Language/Literacy	Problem Solving	Motor Skills
•Count with one to one correspondence. •Complete patterns that have two or more elements. •Sort objects into groups by two or more attributes.	•.Follow three-step directions.	•Engage in problem solving techniques. •Use language to reiterate process and conclusions •Use language to describe objects by a variety of attributes	•N/A

Notes: What did your child do well? Are there any skills they need to continue to work on?

Language Development – Growing our Vocabulary

By Completing Level 3 Activities, We will learn how to...

- Follow three-step directions.
- Use sentences in conversation to describe, explain or predict outcomes of real or imaginary events.
- Initiate and engage in literacy activities.

Literacy Development – Beginning Reading and Writing

By Completing Level 3 Activities, We will learn how to..

- Write their own name, without help.
- Write familiar words by looking at the word then copying.
- Identify all letters by sight and sound

B1. The Name Game - Activity time: 15 minutes

No Materials Needed

Instructions:

Step 1: Sit on the floor or at a table with the child.

Step 2: Explain to them that you're going to spell out some words while making the letter sounds.

Step 3: The adult should clap while you make each letter sound.

Example:
Sun =   /s/   /u/   /n/
(clap) (clap) (clap)

Step 4: Encourage the child to copy the sounds and clap with you. Can they guess what word you sound out?

Step 5: Repeat step 3 and step 4 with the following words:

(clap)	(clap)	(clap)	
/h/	/o/	/t/	= hot
/i/	/c/	/e/	= ice

Step 6: Once they have successfully guessed the previous words, use some other words the child or adult makes up. What do you see around the house that has three letters?
For example: cup and ball.

Optional: If the child is mastering three letter words, the adult can try four letter words.
   Example:

(clap)	(clap)	(clap)	(clap)	
/r/	/a/	/i/	/n/	= rain
/s/	/n/	/o/	/w/	= snow
/b/	/a/	/l/	/l/	= ball

B.1 Learning Objectives

Math/Science	Language/Literacy	Problem Solving	Motor Skills
•Count up to 20 objects, using one to one correspondence.	•Follow three-step directions. •Use sentences in conversation to describe, explain or predict outcomes of real or imaginary events. •Initiate and engage in literacy activities. •Spell familiar words. •Identify all letters by sight and sound	•Use words to discuss predictions •Use language to describe objects by a variety of attributes	•N/A

Notes: What did your child do well? Are there any skills they need to continue to work on?

B2. Hot ABC's - Activity time: 15 minutes

Materials Needed
- ☐ One (1) large piece of cardboard or thick poster paper
- ☐ One (1) bucket or large container
- ☐ One (1) black marker
- ☐ One (1) pair of adult scissors

Instructions:

Step 1: The adult should use a black marker to write each letter of the alphabet (in capital letters) on a piece of cardboard or poster paper. Make sure each letter is evenly spaced apart.

Step 2: The adult should cut each letter out, preferably in the shape of a square, and place the letters in a pile.

Step 3: Put a bucket on the floor and have the child stand 3 feet behind the bucket.

Step 4: Tell the child, "We're going to pretend the letters are **hot**."

Step 5: Ask the child to pick up a letter from the pile. Have them identify the letter by name, then throw it into the bucket as fast as they can! The letters are **"hot"** and may burn if they take too long to name the letter!

Note #1: If the cardboard is too light to throw, glue each letter onto another piece of cardboard.

Note #2: If the child is having a hard time throwing the cardboard, have them pick up the letter from the pile, identify it, then run the letter over to the bucket and put it in. Continue until all letters are in the bucket. Keep track of how long it takes for the child to complete the race.

B.2 Learning Objectives

Math/Science	Language/Literacy	Problem Solving	Motor Skills
•N/A	•Identify all letters by sight and sound •Following Directions	•N/A	•Gross Motor: balance and coordination.

Notes: What did your child do well? Are there any skills they need to continue to work on?

B3. The Very Cold Day - Activity time: 25 minutes

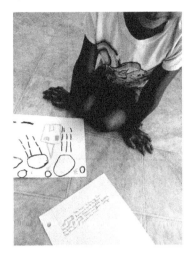

Materials Needed
- ☐ One (1) blank piece of white paper
- ☐ One (1) set of markers or crayons
- ☐ One (1) piece of lined binder paper
- ☐ One (1) pen

Instructions:

Step 1: Tell the child you are going to write a story together.

Step 2: Sit down and say, "It was a very cold day."

Step 3: Ask the child what happened on that cold day. Write down what the child says.

Step 4: When the child is done talking, the adult should continue the story but adding another sentence.

> **Example:**
>
> **Adult:** "It was a very cold day. "
> **Child**: "It was snowing outside."
> **Adult:** "Since it was snowing, I put on my boots and my gloves and went outside."

Step 5: Next, ask the child to continue the story.

Step 6: Continue this pattern until you and the child decide the story is over.

Step 7: When the story is complete, give the child a piece of blank paper and some markers.

Step 8: Instruct the child to draw a picture of the story you just wrote together.

Step 9: When the child is done, ask them to retell the story to you, using the picture they drew.

Step 10: Read the written story to your child

Step 11: Was the child able to retell the story in the correct order?

Step 12: Have your child right their name at the top of the piece of paper

B.3 Learning Objectives

Math/Science	Language/Literacy	Problem Solving	Motor Skills
•N/A	•Write their own name, without help. •Follow directions. •Use sentences in conversation to describe, explain or predict outcomes of real or imaginary events. •Initiate and engage in literacy activities.	•N/A	•Fine Motor: Use a pen or marker to write familiar words.

Notes: What did your child do well? Are there any skills they need to continue to work on?

B4. Wet Words - Activity time: 15 minutes

Materials Needed
☐ One (1) Q-tip
☐ One (1) Small cup of water
☐ One (1) Piece of blank, white paper
☐ One (1) Black Marker

Instructions:

Step 1: The adult should use a black marker to write the following words on a blank piece of paper:

11) Sun
12) Snow
13) Rain
14) Hail
15) Wind
16) Clouds

Step 2: Have the child dip the q-tip in **the cup of water** and trace the letters you wrote.

Step 3: Now the words are wet!

B.4 Learning Objectives

Math/Science	Language/Literacy	Problem Solving	Motor Skills
•N/A	•Follow directions. •Write familiar words by tracing. •Identify all letters by sight and sound	•N/A	•Fine Motor: Trace new words

Notes: What did your child do well? Are there any skills they need to continue to work on?

B5. Snowy Name - Activity time: 15 minutes

Materials Needed
- ☐ One (1) Piece of black construction paper
- ☐ One (1) Piece of white chalk
- ☐ One (1) Pencil
- ☐ One (1) Flashlight
- ☐ Alphabet letter cards (see Step 1 below)
- ☐ Two (2) Pieces of blank, white paper
- ☐ One (1) Pair of adult scissors
- ☐ One (1) Black marker

Instructions:

Step 1: Cut 2 pieces of paper into 2 inch by 2-inch squares.

Step 2: Write the child's name, one letter per square, using upper and lower case letters.

Step 3: Encourage the child to place the cards in order to spell out their whole name?

Step 4: Ask your child to use a pencil to copy each letter onto a black piece of construction paper.

Step 5: Give the child a flashlight and have the child use the flashlight to look at the name (in pencil) they just wrote on the black piece of paper. Can they see it?

Step 6: Ask the child to trace the letters on the black piece of paper with white chalk. Have them say each letter as they write it. Their name is made from snow!

B.5 Learning Objectives

Math/Science	Language/Literacy	Problem Solving	Motor Skills
•N/A	•Write their own name, without help. •Follow directions. •Write familiar words by looking at the word then copying. •Identify all letters by sight and sound	•N/A	•Fine Motor: Use a writing tool to write familiar words. •Fine Motor: Use a pencil to trace new words

Notes: What did your child do well? Are there any skills they need to continue to work on?

Gross Motor – Using our large muscles to move!

By Completing Level 3 Activities, We will learn…

- Participate in a variety of gross motor activities that require balance and coordination.
- Hop on one foot five or more times.

Fine Motor – Using our hands to complete tasks

By Completing Level 3 Activities, We will learn…

- Use scissors to cut out an object.
- Use a pen or marker to write familiar words.
- Use a pencil to trace new words.

C1. Puddle Jump - Activity time: 15 minutes

Materials Needed
☐ Ten (10) Pieces of Blank, Blue Construction Paper
☐ One (1) Roll of Scotch Tape
☐ Child-friendly Music

Instructions:

Step 1: Place two pieces of blue construction paper in a horizontal line, with a three-inch space between each piece of paper. Each piece of paper represents a puddle.

Step 2: Tape two sides of each construction paper onto the floor so they don't move.

Step 3: Turn on some child-friendly music and tell the child to hop on one foot from one piece of paper to the other.

Step 4: Every twenty to thirty seconds stop the music and have the child freeze.

Step 5: When the child freezes, ask the child to say a "weather" word.

   Examples: cold, hot, snow, rain, puddles, etc.

Step 6: After they say the weather word, start the music again.

Step 7: Repeat steps 4 through 6 for at least five minutes.

C.1 Learning Objectives

Math/Science	Language/Literacy	Problem Solving	Motor Skills
•N/A	•Follow auditory and verbal directions. •Use sentences in conversation to describe, explain or predict outcomes of real or imaginary events.	•Use language to describe weather attributes •Demonstrate understanding of differences between people, animals, plants and other parts of the planet.	•Gross Motor: balance and coordination. •Gross Motor: Hop on one foot five or more times.

Notes: What did your child do well? Are there any skills they need to continue to work on?

C2. Spray Bottle Tag - Activity time: 15 minutes

Materials Needed
☐ Two (2) Spray Bottles
☐ Water
☐ Space for running

Instructions:

Step 1: The adult should fill two spray bottles with water.

Step 2: The adult should hold one spray bottle and the child holds the other one.

Step 3: Tell the child you will be playing a game of **Spray Bottle Tag**.

Step 4: When you're in an area that is safe for running, tell the child to chase the adult. When the child catches the adult, they can spray them **three times** (one, two, three) with the spray bottle.

Step 5: Ready, Set, Go! Start running away from the child and encourage them to chase you.

Step 6: Once they catch you, allow them to spray you **three times**. Have them count each spray.

Step 7: Now it's the adult's turn to chase the child.

Step 8: When you catch them, spray them **three times** with the spray bottle.

Step 9: Repeat steps 5 through 8 for at least five minutes.

C.2 Learning Objectives

Math/Science	Language/Literacy	Problem Solving	Motor Skills
•Count using one to one correspondence.	•N/A	•N/A	•Gross Motor: balance and coordination.

Notes: What did your child do well? Are there any skills they need to continue to work on?

C3. Shapely Sun - Activity time: 30 minutes

Materials Needed
- ☐ Two (2) Pieces of Yellow Construction Paper
- ☐ Child-safe Scissors
- ☐ One (1) Glue Stick
- ☐ One (1) Piece of Blue Construction Paper
- ☐ One (1) Pen

Instructions:

Step 1: The adult should use a pen to draw one large circle on a blank piece of **yellow construction paper.**

Step 2: The adult should use a pen to draw **10, one-inch triangles**, on a blank piece of **yellow construction paper.**

Step 3: Allow the child to use child-safe scissors to cut out the shapes.

Step 4: Once the shapes are cut out, give the child one piece of blue construction paper and one glue stick.

Step 5: Direct the child to make a "Sun" with the shapes they cut out. To create the sun, have the child glue the circle in the middle of a piece of blue paper, then glue the triangle shapes around the sun.

Step 6: Allow the child to decorate the sun with a set of markers.

C.3 Learning Objectives

Math/Science	Language/Literacy	Problem Solving	Motor Skills
•Count up to 10 objects, using one to one correspondence. •Describe shapes by at least two characteristics.	•N/A	•N/A	•Fine Motor: Use scissors to cut out an object. •Fine Motor: Use a pencil to draw

Notes: What did your child do well? Are there any skills they need to continue to work on?

C4. Thunder Rolls - Activity time: 20 minutes

Materials Needed
- ☐ One (1) Small empty tin can (empty canned-food container)
- ☐ One (1) Rubber Band
- ☐ One (1) 3"x3" piece of foil
- ☐ Five (5) to Seven (7) Small rocks

Instructions:

Step 1: Have the child collect between **five and seven small rocks,** placing the rocks into the empty tin can.

Step 2: The adult should cover the top of the tin can with a 3" x 3" piece of foil.

Step 3: The adult should place a rubber band on top of the foil, around the tin can, to secure the foil in place.

Step 4: Direct the child to sit across from you on the floor or on the table.

Step 5: Ask the child to demonstrate what thunder sounds like. If you live in an area where they haven't heard thunder or seen lightening before, look for a video on the Internet so that they can see and hear a thunder and lightening storm.

An example of a video is:
EXTREME Close Lightning in HD compilation! Loud thunder! by: Dan Robinson.
https://www.youtube.com/watch?v=Sp9bKDHRfsM

Step 6: The adult should roll the can, filled with rocks, across the floor or the table to the child. Does it sound like thunder?

Step 7: Have the child shake the can **once,** then roll it back to the adult.

Step 8: The adult should shake the can **twice,** then roll it back to the child.

Step 9: The child should shake the can **three** times, then roll it back to the adult.

Step 10: Continue until the adult shakes the can 20 times!

Optional: Ask other family members to join in the game. Thunder rolls!

C.4 Learning Objectives

Math/Science	Language/Literacy	Problem Solving	Motor Skills
•Count up to 20 objects, using one to one correspondence.	•Follow two-step directions.	•Demonstrate understanding of differences between people, animals, plants and other parts of the planet.	•Fine Motor: Eye-hand coordination.

Notes: What did your child do well? Are there any skills they need to continue to work on?

C5. Lightening Balance - Activity time: 15 minutes

Materials Needed
- ☐ One (1) Flashlight
- ☐ One (1) Outside Sidewalk Curb or Balance Beam

Instructions:

Step 1: Ask the child to practice balancing while walking along a curb outside or on a balance beam at the park. Make sure that the curb is in a safe area away from cars.

Step 2: Tell the child the **flashlight** is going to be the **"lighting"** during this game.

Step 3: When the adult shines the flashlight in front of the child's feet, it represents a **"lighting strike"** blocking their path. When this happens, the child must jump off the curb, go around the "light" then step back on the curb. Encourage the child to jump by landing on two feet.

Step 4: The adult should shine the flashlight in front of the child's shoes every four or five steps.

Step 5: To make it a little harder, encourage the child to walk heal-to-toe on the balance beam.

C.5 Learning Objectives

Math/Science	Language/Literacy	Problem Solving	Motor Skills
•N/A	•N/A	•Engage in problem solving techniques.	•Gross Motor: balance and coordination. •Gross Motor: Jumping

Notes: What did your child do well? Are there any skills they need to continue to work on?

Themed Project – Discovering the Elements

Purpose: To teach the process of finding answers to new questions. Each project guides adults and children through investigating specific questions about the theme. The project starts with the development of a hypothesis that is then tested and researched, concluding with an answer to the hypothesis. Specific Learning Objectives include:

Problem Solving Skills: By Completing Level 3, We will learn...

- Predict the results of a familiar action.
- Develop strategies to solve a problem.
- Communicate memories about a sequence of related events that happened in the past.
- Put materials or objects together in new and inventive ways.
- Participate in challenging multi-step activities/projects
- Demonstrate Curiosity and ask Questions.
- Use words to discuss predictions.
- Use language to reiterate process and conclusions.
- Use a variety of techniques to record information and data collection.

Includes: Activities and discussions that address all areas of academic and developmental skills that meets the Level 3 Learning Objectives. Includes math, science, literacy, art, health/safety, gross motor skills, fine motor skills, music and movement and literacy development.

Order of Operation: These projects are designed to be followed in the order they are laid out, each activity building on the knowledge acquired from previous activities.

Project Objective:

When this project is completed, your child should be able to answer the question:

How does water get from the clouds to my sink?

Introduction

Activity #1:

Step 1: Ask the child to draw a picture of how water gets from the clouds in the sky, into their home.

Step 2: When they are done drawing their picture, ask them what they drew and have them explain the process to you.

Step 3: Write down exactly what they say on a separate piece of paper. Make sure to keep this piece of paper on hand to revisit when the project is completed.

Investigation

Section1: Clouds

Discussion: How are clouds formed?

Step 1: Ask the child the following question: How are clouds formed?

Step 2: Listen to what they have to say.

Step 3: Tell them that clouds form when billions of tiny water droplets stick together.

Activity #2 – Cloud formation

Materials Needed
- One (1) Piece of Paper
- One (1) Cup of Elmer's Glue
- One (1) Bottle of blue glitter
- One (1) Elmer's Glue
- One (1) Black Marker

Instructions:

Step 1: Place some Elmer's glue on a piece of paper.

Step 2: Have the child put blue glitter all over the Elmer's glue.

Step 3: Tell the child you are pretending the blue glitter pieces are/represent tiny water droplets.

Step 4: Have the child use a black marker to draw a circle around all of the blue glitter.

Step 5: Tell them all of the tiny water droplets (blue glitter) inside of the circle is a cloud.

> ➤ **Discussion: What do clouds look like?**

Step 1: Ask the child the following question: What do clouds look like?

Step 2: Listen to what they have to say.

Step 3: Read the book: It Looks Like Spilt Milk, by Charles Green Shaw. If you don't have the book, or unable to visit a library, you can use a device that can access the Internet. Watch the story here: **https://www.youtube.com/watch?v=YAx5o286984**

Step 4: If it's a cloudy day, walk outside with the child and look up at the sky. Talk about the shapes that the clouds look like.

> ✏ **Activity #3 – Cloud Creations**

Materials Needed
- Ten (10) Cotton Balls
- One (1) Sheet of white paper
- One (1) Sheet of white tissue paper
- One (1) Sheet of Blue Construction Paper
- One (1) Bottle of Elmer's glue or Glue Stick

Instructions:

Step 1: Put all of the materials on a table in front of the child.

Step 2: Tell the child they can create a variety of clouds using the materials.

Step 3: Encourage them to tear up the tissue paper and white paper into small pieces. They can squish and scrunch them up and then glue them onto the blue construction paper to form a cloud.

> ➤ **Discussion: Are all clouds the same?**

Step 1: Ask the child if they think all the clouds they see are exactly the same.

Step 2: Listen to what they have to say.

Step 3: To demonstrate that no cloud is alike, including their size, use a ruler to measure the length of the clouds that they made in the previous activity (Activity #2).

Step 4: Write down the size of the clouds (in inches) underneath each cloud.

Step 5: Have the child look at all the numbers (sizes). Ask them to show you which one is the biggest. Ask them to show you which one is the smallest.

> ➤ **Discussion: What comes out of a cloud?**

Step 1: Ask the child the following question: What comes out of a cloud?

Step 2: Listen to what they have to say.

Step 3: Tell them water falls out of the cloud, but water turns into a variety of different shapes and textures depending on how cold it is outside. Sometimes water looks like rain, hail or snow.

✎ **Activity #4: Rain, Ice and Snow**

Materials Needed
- One (1) Kitchen thermometer (meat)
- Two (2) Cups of water
- One (1) Refrigerator and Freezer
- One (1) Access to the internet

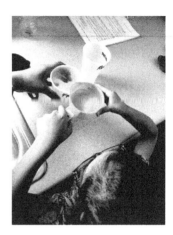

Instructions:

Introduce a kitchen thermometer! Tell the child what all of the numbers and colors mean on the thermometer.

Step 1: Help the child put the kitchen thermometer into the refrigerator. Once it has taken the temperature, take it out and talk about the number (in degrees) with the child.

Step 2: Put the kitchen thermometer into the freezer. Once it has taken the temperature, take it out and talk about the number (in degrees) with the child.

Step 3: Discuss which one is colder. How do they know?

Step 4: The adult should fill up two cups with room temperature water.

Step 5: Place one cup full of water in the refrigerator and the other cup of water in the freezer. Leave them there over night.

Step 6: The next morning, have the child take both cups out and place them on a table.

Step 7: Ask the child what happened to the water?

Step 8: Ask them why they think the water that was in the freezer turned into ice. Was it a colder temperature in the freezer?

Step 9: This tells us that when water gets really cold it freezes – sometimes it turns into snow, other times it is hail.

Step 10: Find a book that talks about all sorts of weather, including rain, snow and hail. If you don't have time to go to the library, please view the book: Maisy's Wonderful Weather Book, by Lucy Cousins, here:

https://www.youtube.com/watch?v=u7pGl1yXpDE&list=PL23nSsgmMbazl8dSb40gHgvPm 2XPWG-tz

✎ **Activity #5: Cooking with Ice – Snow Cones**

Materials Needed
- One (1) Blender
- Ten (10) Ice Cubes
- One (1) Spoon
- One (1) Child-sized cup
- One (1) Pitcher of Kool-aide (pre-made)

Instructions:

Step 1: Tell the child it's very important for everyone to drink lots of water. Water comes in different forms, including ice. We use ice for a lot of things. There are treats that you can make with ice.

Step 2: Place up to ten ice cubes into a blender, snow cone machine or shaved ice machine.

Step 3: Blend the ice cubes until they are small.
** Note: Please make sure that the ice is small enough not to cause a choking hazard for the child.**

Step 4: Once step 2 is completed, scoop the ice out of the machine and place it into a child-sized cup.

Step 5: Pour three or four tablespoons of Kool-aide (any flavor) over the ice.

Step 6: Bon appétit!

Section 2: How does the water from the rain get to my house?

> ➢ **Discussion: Where does the water go once it reaches the ground?**

Step 1: Ask the child the following question: Once the rain has made it onto the ground, and into the lakes, ponds and streams, how does it get to our home?

Step 2: Listen to what they have to say.

Step 3: Watch a video about the water treatment plant. The following YouTube video of the process is a great one:

Water and You, The Water Treatment Process, by New Jersey American Water
https://www.youtube.com/watch?v=tuYB8nMFxQA

Step 4: Tell the child that together, you're going to make a model of the water system.

Step 5: Ask the child what they should use to hold the water in the reservoir? Encourage the children to come up with ideas on their own. Are they going to make something? Are they going to use a bowl? What shape should it be? How big should it be?

Step 6: Next, ask them "Where does the water go after the cloud drops the rain into the reservoirs"?

Step 7: Listen to what they say.

Step 8: Remind them, that when they watched the video, it said that the water flows from the lakes, rivers and streams into plastic pipes, which delivers the water to the water treatment plan.

✎ Activity #6: Water Pipes

Materials Needed
- Items that the child found
- One (1) Pitcher of Water
- One (1) Pen
- One (1) Piece of Plain Paper

Instructions: Have the child search around the home to find items that can be used as a water pipe. It must be something that is strong enough to hold water that's poured into it.

Step 1: Tell the child you are now going to test the items they found to see if they're strong enough to hold the water.

Step 2: Have the child take all of the items they found to the sink.

Step 3: The adult should use a pen to draw a line down the middle of a piece of paper. Write the word "yes" on one side of the paper, and the word "no" on the other side.

Step 4: The adult should use the pitcher filled with water to pour some water onto each item.

Step 5: When each item is tested, write the word of the item in the corresponding section of the chart.
    See example below.

**Example: Items that we tested:

YES (Items that held water)   **NO (Items that did NOT hold water)**
Water Bottle   Black Paper
                                                    Toilet Paper Roll

Step 6: Allow the child to pour the water into each item that was found to test this theory.

** *Note:* *Additional "water pipe" items to test could include an empty two-liter soda bottle, an empty paper towel roll and an empty paper bag.*

➤ **Discussion: What happens to the water that reaches the water sanitation plant?**

Step 1: Ask the child the following question: "What happens to the water once it reaches the water sanitation plant?" Do they remember the steps from the video?

Step 2: Listen to what they have to say.

Step 3: Ask the child the following questions:

- Do they think the water is safe to drink after it reaches the ground?
- Do they think our water is clean to drink after it has been on the ground and in the pipes?
- How does our water become clean? Who cleans it? How does it happen?
- What happens to the water once it reaches the sanitation plant?

Step 4: Tell them that you are going to demonstrate how the sanitation plant cleans the water.

✎ Activity #7: Water Sanitization

Materials Needed
- One (1) Bucket
- One (1) Gallon of Water
- One (1) Handful of rocks
- One (1) Handful of leaves/weeds
- One (1) Cup of sand
- One (1) Child sand sifter or kitchen water colander
- Four (4) Drops of blue food coloring
- One (1) Wooden Spoon
- One (1) Child's magnifying glass

Instructions:

Step 1: First, the water enters into the water sanitation plant and goes through large screens to remove large rocks, twigs and leaves.

Show the child how this process is completed by filling up a bucket with water, sand, rocks and weeds. The adult should demonstrate how to use a sifter to sift out the items from the water. Allow the child a turn to do this.

Step 2: Tell the child that after the twigs and sticks are removed, coagulant (a liquid chemical) is added to the water to kill any bacteria. The water then flows into a large basin where it is slowly stirred by large paddles.

 To demonstrate this, add one or two drops of blue watercolor/food color to the water to make it look like chemicals. Give the child a wooden spoon and encourage them to stir the water quickly.

Step 3: Next, tell them the water moves into another area called a "gravity" filter.

Show the child how this works by placing the clean rocks (from the materials list) into the sand sifter. Pour the blue water from Step 2 over the rocks, catching the water with a bucket below. This is what makes the dirty water clean.

Step 4: Next, chlorine is added to kill any disease causing bacteria. The total treatment process takes five to eight hours.

The adult should add a couple more drops of food color to the water in the bucket to represent chlorine.

Step 5: Now the water is clean! Place plastic measuring cups and magnifying glasses into the bucket of "clean" water, so the child can look at the water to see if it looks safe to drink.

Step 6: Ask the child if they can repeat the water sanitation process from start to finish? Allow them to use the tools and see if they remember the process.

> ➢ **Discussion: Now that the water is clean, how does it get to our home?**

Step 1: Ask the child the following question: "Where does the water go after it is cleaned"? Do they remember the steps from the video?

Step 2: Listen to what they have to say.

Step 3: Tell them the water leaves the treatment plant through more tubes and is stored in covered reservoirs until it's needed.

✎ Activity #8:

Materials Needed
- One (1) Empty cardboard box
- One (1) Pair of Adult sized scissors
- Eight (8) or more empty water bottles
- One (1) Roll off duct tape.
- One (1) Box of children's markers

Instructions:

Step 1: Use a Tupperware bowl to represent a reservoir. Put the bowl at the end of the "water sanitation" system from Activity #6. Remind the child that this reservoir must have a lid to make sure the water stays clean.

Step 2: When anyone turns the water on, the pipes suck the water out of the reservoir. The water flows through the pipe path to a faucet. The adult should cut the ends off of some empty plastic water bottles and tape them together to make a pipeline for the water to run through.

Step 3: Now it is time to make a sink! Allow the child to use crayons/markers/stickers to decorate a large cardboard box. Next, the adult should cut holes out of the box to make a space for the faucet. Attach the water bottles to the hole on the box to represent the pipes that attach to the faucet, which allows water to flow.

Section 3:Water Conservation

✎ Activity #9:

Step 1: Now that the child knows where the water comes from and the long process it takes to get clean, discuss with them why it's important to conserve water.

Step 2: Ask them "What would happen if we ran out of water?"

Step 3: Watch the short video: The Water Song by Sesame Street:
https://www.youtube.com/watch?v=CwpHMPH-WbM

Conclusion: Memory and Knowledge

✎ Activity #10: Summarization

Materials Needed
- One (1) Piece of Blank White Paper
- One (1) Pack of Markers or Crayons
- One (1) Piece of Lined Binder Paper
- One (1) Pen

Instructions:

Step 1: Tell the child they are now going to have an opportunity to draw a picture of how water gets from the clouds to their house.

Step 2: Allow them to draw the picture using markers or crayons.

Step 3: When they have finished, the adult should have a pen and piece of lined binder paper.

Step 4: Ask the child to tell the story, using the picture they drew, of how the water gets from the clouds to the sky.

Step 5: The adult should write down exactly what the child says, on the piece of paper.

After you are finished with this project, ask the child if they want to know anything else about water. You may be surprised about their answers! Write them down and encourage them to read books and to find videos to find the answers to their questions.

Recommended Weather Songs:

'Rain, Rain Go Away'
By Unknown

Rain, rain, go away
Come again some other day
We want to go outside and play
Come again some other day.

'It's Raining, It's Pouring'
By Unknown

It's raining, it's pouring;
The old man is snoring.
He went to bed and he
Bumped his head
And he couldn't get up in the morning.

'If All the Raindrops'
By Barney

If all the raindrops
Were lemon drops and gumdrops
Oh, what a rain that would be!
Standing outside, with my mouth open wide
Ah, ah, ah, ah, ah, ah, ah, ah, ah, ah
If all the raindrops
Were lemon drops and gumdrops
Oh, what a rain that would be!

If all the snowflakes
Were candy bars and milkshakes
Oh, what a snow that would be!
Standing outside, with my mouth open wide
Ah, ah, ah, ah, ah, ah, ah, ah, ah, ah
If all the snowflakes
Were candy bars and milkshakes
Oh, what a snow that would be!

If all the sunbeams
Were bubblegum and ice cream
Oh, what a sun that would be!
Standing outside, with my mouth open wide
Ah, ah, ah, ah, ah, ah, ah, ah, ah, ah
If all the sunbeams
Were bubblegum and ice cream
Oh, what a sun that would be!

....

Thanks for playing! See you in the next Unit:
Pre-K Your Way - Level 3, Unit 4
Planet Earth

Pre-K YOUR Way

Level 3 Unit 4

Planet Earth
Earth's Layers Project

Planet Earth Themed Items For Indoor Learning Environment

Now that you have set up your environment, you are ready to place materials in it that directly relate to the theme you are studying! Here are some suggestions of materials your child can free-play with during the "Exploring My Community" Theme:

Books: Age-appropriate books that directly correlate with the monthly theme can be found at your local library or bought separately online. This is a great opportunity to take a trip with your child to your local library and go on a search together. Have them identify words or pictures on the cover of children's books that correlate to the theme. Place a variety of books related to the theme in your child's book area. This will increase opportunities for them to expand their knowledge and use what they learn in the activities to comprehend what they read in the books.

Art Area: Encourage your child use this throughout each day by rotating items in an art area. These can be items have already been painted on, paper that they drew on already or leftover materials from another project. Thought provoking art projects are created when children are given unlimited opportunities to explore a variety of materials.

Some suggestions for the art area include:
- Crayons
- Paper
- Pens
- Empty Boxes (all kinds)
- Empty Toilet Paper or Paper Towel Rolls
- Foil
- Clean Q-tips for painting
- Scraps of paper
- Scraps of Yarn
- Scraps of any type of material – including fabric, sand paper, etc.
- Paper Bags
- Straws
- Popsicle Sticks
- Anything else that can be reused.

Suggested Cooking Activities

These are simple cooking and snack-time activities that correlate with the theme. The children can prepare these snacks with adult assistance.

1) Up and Down - Mountains and Canyons:

Place one cup of yogurt into a bowl and put three graham crackers on a child's plate. Ask the child to use a spoon to scoop a hole out of the yogurt. This hole is a canyon, just like the Grand Canyon. Allow them to form a "mountain" with the graham crackers on the plate. How tall of a "mountain" can they create?

2) Land and Water:

The adult should make a batch of blue Jell-O. Place the entire Jell-O liquid into one large Tupperware container. Once the Jell-O has solidified, allow the child to make a "land" island out of vanilla wafers. Encourage them to put the "land masses" (vanilla wafers) into the water ("Jell-O") and make landmasses throughout the "world" (the Tupperware container). Once the child is done, encourage them to tell you about each land mass. Why did they placed it in that spot and who lives on each one.

Sensory Bin Suggestions

A sensory bin is a small plastic bucket that is filled with a variety of materials. Sensory bins provide a space to engage in sensory-rich activities that offer opportunities to investigate textures while providing activities for relaxation and self-regulation. Sensory bins encourage language development, small motor development and control, spatial concepts, problem-solving skills and scientific observations. Each month there are suggested sensory bin materials that correlate with the theme of the unit.

Set Up Instructions: In a Plastic Bucket, rotate the following sensory activities throughout the month.

1) **Dirt and Mud Name Exploration:**

   Place four to five cups of dirt in a small plastic bin. Encourage the child to use a magnifying glass to investigate all aspects of the dirt and what it's made of. Encourage the child to use a pencil, Q-tip, their finger or the back side of a paintbrush to write their name in the dirt
   a. *Optional: Allow the child to add water to the dirt and make mud. Is it easier to write letters in mud or sand?*
   b. *Optional: After the child writes their name in the sand, allow the child to use small rocks to outline the letters they made in the sand.*

2) **Leaves and Weeds:**

   Nature is all around us. On the ground, there are leaves that fall from trees and there are weeds that grow in the grass. Encourage the child to gather up to 10 leaves and pick 10 weeds. Have them place the weeds and leaves into the sensory bin. A lot of small animals use these leaves and weeds as shelter. The adult should place 7 raisins in the sensory bin to represent the bugs that hide under the leaves and weeds. Throughout the week, encourage the child to build homes and a community for the bugs (raisins) in the bin.

Dramatic Play Area

This play area allows children to understand and experience the adult world through imitation and creativity. The dramatic play area provides a safe space for young children to create stories while practicing new vocabulary and practicing social skills. It is also a space where groups of children engage in pretend play which provides opportunities to learn self-help skills, share space and materials, take turns and the use abstract thinking. Each month there is a list of suggested materials to integrate into this area, which correlate with the theme of the month.

Suggested props to include in the dramatic play/pretend play area include:

- Maps of Local Parks
- Maps of the World
- Globe
- Pictures of different areas of the world
- Pictures and books of flowers
- Pictures and books of a variety of animals (including land and sea animals)
- Pictures and books of a variety of national parks
- Small plastic people
- Buckets/Pails/Sand Shovels/Dirt
- A variety of objects that are in the shape of a Circle
- Hiking shoes and boots
- An area where children can pretend to climb mountains, looks down into canyons and run from lava flow
- Play Camera
- Binoculars

Learning Objectives - Level 3

After completing all modules in the Level 3 Curriculum Series, the child should be able to:

Mathematics
- Solve simple addition and subtractions problems with objects.
- Count up to 20 objects, using one to one correspondence.
- Recognizes the names of Numerals.
- Understands size words (Smaller vs. Larger).
- Describe shapes by at least two characteristics.
- Complete patterns that have two or more elements.
- Sort objects into groups by two or more attributes.
- Show understanding of measurement by using measuring tools.

Science
- Demonstrate Curiosity and ask Questions
- Engage in problem solving techniques.
- Use words to discuss predictions
- Use language to reiterate process and conclusions
- Use a variety of techniques to record information and data collection
- Use language to describe objects by a variety of attributes
- Demonstrate understanding of differences between people, animals, plants and other parts of the planet.
- Complete multi-step projects.

Language and Literacy
- Write their own name, without help.
- Follow three-step directions.
- Use sentences in conversation to describe, explain or predict outcomes of real or imaginary events.
- Initiate and engage in literacy activities.
- Write familiar words by looking at the word then copying.
- Identify all letters by sight and sound

Problem Solving Skills
- Predict the results of a familiar action.
- Develop strategies to solve a problem.
- Communicate memories about a sequence of related events that happened in the past.
- Put materials or objects together in new and inventive ways.
- Participate in challenging multi-step activities.

Gross Motor/Fine Motor Development
- Participate in a variety of gross motor activities that require balance and coordination.
- Hop on one foot five or more times.
- Use scissors to cut out an object.
- Use a pen or marker to write familiar words.
- Use a pencil to trace new words

Part 1: Planet Earth Themed Activities

These activities have been developed to meet specific, age-appropriate, Kindergarten-Readiness skills. These skills are specified in the learning objectives of each activity. The following activities may be completed in any order desired and are specifically designed to address the academic domains: math, science, language, literacy, cognitive, problem solving, and physical development.

Each activity is on its own page. If the adult chooses to print the activities, the space below each activity is provided for adults to write notes regarding the activity. Adults are encouraged to note if the child enjoyed the activity and if the child needs to work on specific learning objectives. Each activity can be repeated more than once to enable the child to master the learning objectives designed for that activity.

A. Math/Science Development

1. Volcanoes
2. Grand Canyon
3. Glaciers
4. Mountain Climbing – Mt. Everest
5. Oceans, Lakes and Rivers Connect

B. Language/Literacy Development

1. Fan the Wind
2. My Very Long Journey
3. Exploring Directions
4. Inside a RIVER
5. The Oldest Tree

C. Physical Development- Gross Motor & Fine-Motor

1. Recycle Builder
2. Pattern Cycle
3. Trash Throw
4. Up, Down, Left and Right
5. Land, Earth and Water

Mathematical Development – Understanding Numbers and their Purpose

By Completing Level 3 Activities, We will learn how to...

- o Solve simple addition and subtractions problems with objects.
- o Count up to 20 objects, using one to one correspondence.
- o Recognizes the names of Numerals.
- o Understands size words (Smaller vs. Larger).
- o Describe shapes by at least two characteristics.
- o Complete patterns that have two or more elements.
- o Sort objects into groups by two or more attributes.
- o Show understanding of measurement by using measuring tools.

Science/Cognitive Development – Learning How to Solve Problems

By Completing Level 3 Activities, We will learn how to..

- o Demonstrate Curiosity and ask Questions
- o Engage in problem solving techniques.
- o Use words to discuss predictions
- o Use language to reiterate process and conclusions
- o Use a variety of techniques to record information and data collection
- o Use language to describe objects by a variety of attributes
- o Demonstrate understanding of differences between people, animals, plants and other parts of the planet.
- o Complete multi-step projects.

✎ A1. Volcanoes - Activity time: 15 minutes

Materials Needed
- ☐ One (1) Tub of Red Playdough
- ☐ One (1) Tub of Brown Playdough
- ☐ One (1) Tape Measure or Ruler
- ☐ One (1) Blank piece of white paper.
- ☐ One (1) Pen
- ☐ One (1) Baking Pan
- ☐ One (1) Piece of parchment paper.

Instructions:

Step 1: The adult should place a large piece of parchment paper on top of a baking pan/cookie sheet.

Step 2: Have the child take the brown play dough out of the container and build a mountain out of it.

Step 3: Explain to the child that some mountains are volcanoes. They have red lava in them, which is made up of Magma. Magma is combination of crystals, volcanic glass and bubbles. Show them a video of a volcano erupting.

You can search online for a video like the following: Volcano Erupting by watch3rboy
https://www.youtube.com/watch?v=R0Zbj7S22zs

Step 4: Tell the child they are going to make a volcano erupt with lava. Have them make a tall lava spout with the red play dough, placing it on top of the volcano.

Step 5: Use a tape measure or ruler to assist the child in **measuring how tall** their lava spout (eruption) is. Explain to the child that the **highest lava eruption** recorded is between **1,000 and 2,000 feet!**

Step 6: Have the child write down the numbers (in inches) of **how tall their volcano eruption is.**

Step 7: Can they make another eruption that is taller? Allow them to use items around your home that will help the volcano grow in height (such as empty paper towel rolls). Encourage them to continue measuring and writing down how tall the volcano is.

A.1 Learning Objectives

Math/Science	Language/Literacy	Problem Solving	Motor Skills
• Solve simple addition and subtractions problems with objects. • Recognizes the names of Numerals. • Understands size words (Smaller vs. Larger). • Show understanding of measurement by using measuring tools.	• N/A	• Demonstrate Curiosity and ask Questions • Use a variety of techniques to record information and data collection • Use language to describe objects by a variety of attributes	• Fine Motor: Use a pen or marker to write familiar words and

Notes: What did your child do well? Are there any skills they need to continue to work on?

A2. Grand Canyon - Activity time: 15 minutes

Materials Needed
- ☐ One (1) Package of Crayons or Markers
- ☐ Two (2) Pieces of paper, taped together.
- ☐ One (1) Blank Piece of Lined Paper

Instructions:

Step 1: Ask the child what they would need to have in order to make a large hole in the ground? **Example:** A shovel or a tractor.

Tell them they are going to investigate one of the deepest holes in the United States called the Grand Canyon. The Grand Canyon is 277 miles (446 km) **long**, up to 18 miles (29 km) **wide** and is over a mile (6,093 feet) **deep**.

Step 2: Using a tape measure, measure how tall the child is (in feet).

Step 3: Ask the child to draw a picture of themselves on the piece of paper with the crayons. Help the child write the numbers (in feet) of how tall they, are on the photo they drew.

Step 4: Using a tape measure, measure how tall the adult is (in feet).

Step 5: Ask the child to draw a picture of the adult on the piece of paper with the crayons. Help the child write the numbers (in feet) how tall the adult is, next to the picture of the adult.

Step 6: Ask the child: Who **is taller**, the adult or the child?

Step 7: Ask the child to draw a picture of a swimming pool.

Step 8: Tell them the deep end of a swimming pool is usually about **12 feet deep**. Help them write the number 12 next to the swimming pool.

Step 9: Using a new sheet of paper, ask the child to draw a picture of the **Grand Canyon**, a **deep hole in the earth**.

Step 9: Next to their picture, help them write the **number 6,093 feet**. That is a very **BIG** number!

Step 10: Watch a video online of the Grand Canyon to see its depth. The following video is an example. It's a video from a helicopter flying over the grand canyon:

Grand Canyon Helicopter Flight by Hoosier Time's Travel Videos
https://www.youtube.com/watch?v=UT3hQlY4oek

A.2 Learning Objectives

Math/Science	Language/Literacy	Problem Solving	Motor Skills
• Recognizes the names of Numerals. • Understands size words (Smaller vs. Larger). • Describe shapes by at least two characteristics. • Show understanding of measurement by using measuring tools.	• Use sentences in conversation to describe, explain or predict outcomes of real or imaginary events.	• Demonstrate Curiosity and ask Questions • Engage in problem solving techniques. • Use words to discuss predictions • Use a variety of techniques to record information and data collection • Use language to describe objects by a variety of attributes	• Fine Motor: Use a pen or marker to write familiar words and numbers.

Notes: What did your child do well? Are there any skills they need to continue to work on?

A3. Glaciers - Activity time: 20 minutes

Materials Needed
- ☐ Twenty Four (24) ice cubes
- ☐ One (1) cookie sheet/baking pan
- ☐ One (1) piece of parchment paper
- ☐ One (1) Thermometer or Digital Food Thermometer

Instructions:

Step 1: Tell the child there are **large blocks of ice on earth** called **Glaciers**. These ice blocks are very tall and they help keep that ocean waters cool.

Step 2: Place a cookie sheet/baking pan in front of the child and place the parchment paper on top.

Step 3: Place **24 ice cubes** onto the baking sheet.

Step 4: Ask them to build the tallest tower that they can.

Step 5: Ask them to describe what they feel when the touch the ice cubes (slimy, cold, wet, etc).

Step 6: Using a thermometer, show the child how to measure temperature of the ice. (Place the thermometer next to the ice cube and have your child help you read the temperature.) BRRRRR!

Step 7: Check your home thermostat to find out what the temperature is in your home.

Step 8: Ask the child and see if they can tell you which number is higher (the ice temperature OR the house temperature). Tell them that whichever number is higher, is warmer.

Step 9: Next, have the child use the ice cubes to build a long train. Encourage addition and subtraction concepts by asking them to complete the following:

a) Make a train with five ice cubes, now take away two. How many do you have left?

b) Make a train with seven ice cubes, now add four. How many do you have?

c) Make a train with fifteen ice cubes, now take away eleven. How many do you have left?

d) Make a train with one ice cube, now add fifteen. How many do you have?

A.3 Learning Objectives

Math/Science	Language/Literacy	Problem Solving	Motor Skills
•Solve simple addition and subtractions problems with objects. •Count up to 20 objects, using one to one correspondence. •Recognizes the names of Numerals. •Describe shapes by at least two characteristics. •Show understanding of measurement by using measuring tools.	•Follow three-step directions. •Use sentences in conversation to describe, explain or predict outcomes of real or imaginary events.	•Demonstrate Curiosity and ask Questions •Use words to discuss predictions •Use language to reiterate process and conclusions •Use a variety of techniques to record information and data collection •Use language to describe objects by a variety of attributes	•Fine Motor: Use a pen or marker to write familiar words and numbers •Fine Motor: Using advanced grasp to build with small objects.

Notes: What did your child do well? Are there any skills they need to continue to work on?

A4. Mount Everest - Activity time: 10 minutes
(Complete Activity A2- prior to completing this activity)

Materials Needed
- ☐ Three (3) pieces of paper
- ☐ One (1) pen
- ☐ One (1) yellow highlighter
- ☐ One (1) tape measure

Instructions:

Step 1: Ask the child if they remember how deep the Grand Canyon is? **(6,093 feet)**

Step 2: Help the child tape **three pieces of paper** together to make a very **tall piece of paper**.

Step 3: Now you're going to find out how tall the highest mountain in the world is. **The Mountain is called Mount Everest. It is 29,029 feet tall.** Tell them that you are going to find out if **Mount Everest will fit into the Grand Canyon**.

Step 4: Using a ruler or tape measure, help the child **measure 6 inches**, starting from the bottom of the paper you just taped together. Have them make a line that is 6 inches tall. **Tell them the Grand Canyon is 6 thousand feet tall.**

____ 6,093

Step 5: Help the child write the number 6,093 next to the line.

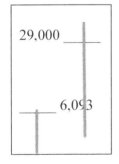

29,000 ____

6,093 ____

Step 6: Using a ruler or tape Measure, help the child measure **29 inches tall.** Start the line at the bottom of the paper. Have them make a line that is 29 inches tall next to the line from Step 4. Tell the child that **Mt. Everest is 29 thousand feet tall.**

Step 7: Help the child write the number 29 next to the line that is 29 inches tall.

Step 8: Tell the child to look at the two lines, one is how deep the Grand Canyon is and the other is **how tall Mt. Everest is.** Ask the child if they think that Mt. Everest can fit into the Grand Canyon.

Step 8: Mt. Everest is too tall to fit into the Grand Canyon. There are a lot of numbers between six and 29.

Step 9: Encourage the child to make a small tally line on the piece of paper for every number between 6 and 29.

7 8 9 10 11 12 13 14 15 16 17 18 19 20 21 22 23 24 25 26 27 28 29
1 1 1 1 1 1 1 1 1 1 1 1 1 1 1 1 1 1 1 1 1 1 1

There are **23** Tally's!

Step 10: Now ask the child to count how many tally lines they drew (Answer: 23).

Step 11: That means that **Mt. Everest is twenty three thousand feet taller** than the Grand Canyon.

Step 12: If you would like, find a video on the internet to see how tall Mt. Everest is.

A.4 Learning Objectives

Math/Science	Language/Literacy	Problem Solving	Motor Skills
• Solve simple addition and subtractions problems with objects. • Count up to 20 objects, using one to one correspondence. • Recognizes the names of Numerals. • Understands size words (Smaller vs. Larger). • Show understanding of measurement by using measuring tools.	• .Follow three-step directions. • Use sentences in conversation to describe, explain or predict outcomes of real or imaginary events.	• Demonstrate Curiosity and ask Questions • Engage in problem solving techniques. • Use words to discuss predictions • Use language to reiterate process and conclusions • Use a variety of techniques to record information and data collection • Use language to describe objects by a variety of attributes. • Complete Multi-Step Projects	• Fine Motor: Use a pen or marker to write familiar words and numbers.

Notes: What did your child do well? Are there any skills they need to continue to work on?

A5. Ocean and Land - Activity time: 20 minutes

Materials Needed
☐ Seven (7) pieces of blue construction paper
☐ Three (3) pieces of brown construction paper
☐ One (1) yellow highlighter
☐ One (1) black pen or marker
☐ One (1) roll of tape

Instructions:

Step 1: Explain to the child you're going to discover how much of planet earth is covered in water.

Step 2: Tell the child the Earth is covered **with 70% water**. The rest of the earth is called land, which is what people live on.

Step 3: Together, you and the child are going to find out how much 70% is. Have the child count how many pieces of brown paper there are (Answer: 1, 2, 3). There are **three pieces** of brown paper.

Step 4: Ask the child count how many pieces of blue paper there are (Answer: 1, 2, 3, 4, 5, 6, 7). There are seven pieces of blue paper.

Step 5: Ask the child if they can tell you which number is **larger**.

Step 6: Next, the adult should use the **yellow highlighter** to write the number (1 through 3) on the brown pieces of paper. One number should be written on each piece of paper.

Step 7: Next, the adult should use the **yellow highlighter** to write the number (1 through 7) on the blue pieces of paper. One number should be written on each piece of paper.

Step 8: Direct the child to use a black pen or marker to trace each number.

Step 9: Ask the child to tell you which **color** has the **most** pieces of paper (**Answer:** The blue paper).

Step 10: Next, have the child line up the blue pieces of paper **and** the brown pieces of paper in a **horizontal line**.

Step 11: Ask the child to count how many **total pieces of paper** there are (1...10). **There are ten pieces of paper.**

Step 12: Ask the child: "How many pieces of paper are brown (3)?" Answer: There are **three pieces** of brown paper. The brown pieces of paper represent how much land there is on the earth.

Step 13: Next, ask the child how many pieces of paper are blue (Answer: 7). There are seven pieces of blue paper. The blue pieces of paper represent how much water there is on the earth.

Step 14: Next explain to the child that 7 out of 10 pieces of paper are blue. That means that seventy percent of the pieces of paper are blue. Since the blue paper represents water, seventy percent of the earth is made up of water.

Step 15: Next explain to the child that 3 out of 10 pieces of paper are brown. That means that thirty percent of the pieces of paper are brown. Since the brown paper represents land, thirty percent of the earth is made up of land.

Step 16: Ask the child if the number **30** or **70** is bigger. Answer: 7 is a larger number so 70 is the larger number.

Step 17: Allow the child to tape all the blue pieces of paper together.

Step 18: Allow the child to tape all the brown pieces of paper together.

Step 19: The adult should use a black marker to write the number 30 on the blue pieces of paper.

Step 20: The adult should use a black marker to write the number 70 on the brown pieces of paper.

Step 21: Ask the child which percentage is larger, **70 percent** or **30 percent**.

Step 22: There is more blue paper than brown paper, so there is more water on planet earth than there is land.

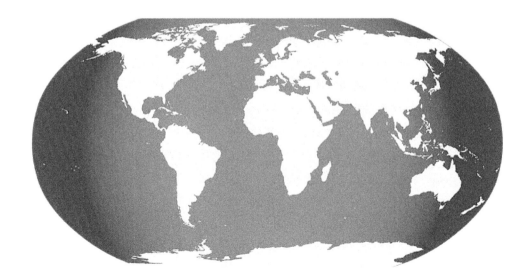

A.5 Learning Objectives

Math/Science	Language/Literacy	Problem Solving	Motor Skills
•Solve simple addition and subtraction problems with objects. •Count up to 20 objects, using one to one correspondence. •Recognizes the names of Numerals. •Understands size words (Smaller vs. Larger). •Show understanding of measurement by using measuring tools.	•Follow three-step directions. •Use sentences in conversation to describe, explain or predict outcomes of real or imaginary events.	•Demonstrate Curiosity and ask Questions •Engage in problem solving techniques. •Use words to discuss predictions •Use language to reiterate process and conclusions •Use a variety of techniques to record information and data collection •Use language to describe objects by a variety of attributes •Demonstrate understanding of differences between people, animals, plants and other parts of the planet. •Complete multi-step projects.	•N/A

Notes: What did your child do well? Are there any skills they need to continue to work on?

Language Development – Growing our Vocabulary

By Completing Level 3 Activities, We will learn how to...

- o Follow three-step directions.
- o Use sentences in conversation to describe, explain or predict outcomes of real or imaginary events.
- o Initiate and engage in literacy activities.

Literacy Development – Beginning Reading and Writing

By Completing Level 3 Activities, We will learn how to..

- o Write their own name, without help.
- o Write familiar words by looking at the word then copying.
- o Identify all letters by sight and sound

B1. Fan The Wind - Activity time: 15 minutes

Materials Needed
- ☐ One (1) Straw
- ☐ Two (1) Pieces of paper
- ☐ One (1) Yellow highlighter
- ☐ One (1) Black Pen

Instructions:

Step 1: Tell the child it is time to investigate the **wind.**

Step 2: Ask the child if they can **see** the wind.

Step 3: Since they can't see the wind, ask the child if it is it real? How do they know? Use a pen to write down what the child says on one piece of paper.

Step 4: Tell the child they are going to **be the Wind**.

Step 5: Have the child crumple up one piece of paper into a ball.

Step 6: Have the child blow air through the straw.

Step 7: Ask the child to put their hand at the end of the straw and see if they can feel their breath.

Step 8: Ask the child if their breath is real. Why? Answer: It's real because you can feel it.

Step 9: Have the child point one end of the straw towards the crumpled piece of paper and blow air through it. Does the crumpled piece of paper move around the room?

Step 10: Ask the child how the piece of paper could move if they couldn't see **the "wind"** they were making.

Step 11: Ask the child to tell you about the wind and write down what they say (on the piece of paper from Step 3).

Step 12: Have the child write their name on the piece of paper. (If the child is unable to write their name on their own yet, the adult should write it in a yellow highlighter and have the child trace the letters).

B.1 Learning Objectives

Math/Science	Language/Literacy	Problem Solving	Motor Skills
•N/A	•Write their own name, without help. •Use sentences in conversation to describe, explain or predict outcomes of real or imaginary events.	•Demonstrate Curiosity and ask Questions •Engage in problem solving techniques. •Use words to discuss predictions •Use language to reiterate process and conclusions •Use language to describe objects by a variety of attributes •Demonstrate understanding of differences between people, animals, plants and other parts of the planet.	•Fine Motor: Use a pen or marker to write familiar words.

Notes: What did your child do well? Are there any skills they need to continue to work on?

B2. My Very, Very Long Journey - Activity time: 15 minutes
  (Complete Activities A1 through A5 prior to completing this activity)

Materials Needed
  ☐ One (1) large piece of blank paper
  ☐ One (1) pen
  ☐ One (1) package of markers or crayons
  ☐ One (1) blank piece of lined paper

Instructions:

Step 1: Have the child think back to all of the mountains, volcanos, rivers and canyons they investigated in Section A activities. Ask them if they can remember **how tall Mt. Everest is.**

Step 2: It's time to **create a story about a very, very, long journey that your family will be taking.** With a pen and blank paper, have an adult write down the child's answers to the following questions:

- What journey around the Earth should we go on as a family?
- Where are we going to start?
- Where are we going to end?
- What are we going to see?
- What happens after we get into our car?

Step 3: Give the child a blank sheet of paper and some crayons or markers. Tell the child to draw a picture of the family journey they just described.

Step 4: Ask the child to explain the picture. Were they able to recreate the journey they told you?

Step 5: Ask your child to write their name on the paper.

Step 6: Ask your child to use a pen to trace their answers to the questions from Step 2. Can they identify each letter as they trace it? Do they know the sound of each letter?

Step 7: Keep the story to revisit later.

B.2 Learning Objectives

Math/Science	Language/Literacy	Problem Solving	Motor Skills
•Understands size words (Smaller vs. Larger).	•Write their own name, without help. •Use sentences in conversation to describe, explain or predict outcomes of real or imaginary events. •Initiate and engage in literacy activities. •Write familiar words by looking at the word then copying. •Identify all letters by sight and sound	•Use words to discuss predictions •Use language to reiterate process and conclusions •Use language to describe objects by a variety of attributes •Demonstrate understanding of differences between people, animals, plants and other parts of the planet.	•Fine Motor: Use a pen or marker to write familiar words. •Fine Motor: Use a pencil to trace new words

Notes: What did your child do well? Are there any skills they need to continue to work on?

B3. Exploring Directions - Activity time: 15 minutes

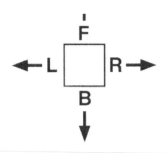

Materials Needed
- One (1) outdoor sidewalk area
- Two (2) pieces of sidewalk chalk (each one a different color)

Instructions:

Step 1: Tell the child this activity teaches how to **following directions** on a map.

Step 2: Using a piece of sidewalk chalk, the adult should draw a square, ⬜ large enough for the child to stand inside of.

Step 3: Using a piece of sidewalk chalk, the adult should write the letter:

- **"R"** to the **right** of the square and then an arrow pointing to the right (see photo above).

- **"L"** to the **left** of the square and then an arrow pointing to the left (see photo above).

- **"F"** above the square and then an arrow pointing **forward (up)** (see photo above).

- **"B"** below the square and then an arrow pointing **backwards (down)** (see photo above).

Step 4: Have the child repeat the phrase "I can jump Forward, Backwards, Left and Right".

Step 5: Ask the child trace the letters and the arrows with a new color of sidewalk chalk.

Step 6: Tell the child to stand in the middle of the square. Tell them that **directions are important** when going on a walk or following a trail through the mountains.

Step 7: Tell the child that he/she must listen to the **word** you say and **jump** on the letter that represents that word. For Example: When the adult says **"left",** the child should jump on the letter **"L".)**

Step 8: The adult should say the following words, in order, asking the child jump on the corresponding letter.

- Forward (F) , Backward (B), Left (L), and Right (R)

- Right (R), Forward (F), Left (L), Backward (B)

- Right (R), Right (R), Left (L), Left (L), Forward (F)

- Backward (B), Backward (B), Left (L), Forward (F)

Step 9: Repeat Step 8 asking your child to Hop (on one foot) instead of Jump.

Step 10: Ask the child to make up a **two or three step**, **repetitive pattern**. The means that there are **two or three letters in each pattern**. Ask the child to name each letter and what direction it stands for.

For Example:
- F, F, B, B

- F, L, B, F, L, B

Step 11: Have another child or adult practice jumping on the corresponding letter while the child says the name of the direction.

B.3 Learning Objectives

Math/Science	Language/Literacy	Problem Solving	Motor Skills
• Complete patterns that have two or more elements. • Sort objects into groups by two or more attributes. • Show understanding of measurement by using measuring tools.	• Follow three-step directions. • Write familiar words by looking at the word then copying. • Identify all letters by sight and sound	• Understanding Visual and Auditory Symbols.	• Gross Motor: balance and coordination. • Gross Motor: Hop on one foot five or more times. • Fine Motor: Use a pen or marker to write familiar words. • Fine Motor: Use a pencil to trace new words

Notes: What did your child do well? Are there any skills they need to continue to work on?

✎ B4. Inside a River - Activity time: 15 minutes

Materials Needed
- ☐ One (2) Pieces of White Construction Paper
- ☐ One (1) Small container of Blue Washable Paint
- ☐ One (1) Paper Plate
- ☐ One (1) Q-Tip
- ☐ One (1) Black Pen
- ☐ One (1) Yellow Highlighter

Instructions:

Step 1: Tell the child there is a lot of water on planet Earth. Do they remember how much of the earth is covered in water (Activity A5 – 70%)?

Step 2: Ask the child: "Do you know what the areas of water are called on planet earth?"
Answer: rivers, streams, creeks, lakes and oceans.

Step 3: Tell the child they are going to have the opportunity to make **their own river**.
Ask them: "Do you know what a river looks like?"

Step 4: Discuss what a river is:

- It's a place where there is flowing water.

- Rivers are often curvy and not straight.

- They go in all directions including left, right, forward and sometimes backwards.

- Lots of things live in rivers including animals and plants.

Step 5: The adult should put two tablespoons of blue, non-toxic, washable paint onto a paper plate.

Step 6: Place the paper plate next to one piece of **White Construction paper**.

Step 7: Tell the child they can make their own squiggly river on the paper using the Q-tip and the blue paint. The child can dip one end of the Q-tip in the paint and paint their river.

Step 8: Ask the child the following questions about their river. On a second piece of paper, use a yellow highlighter to write down the child's answers to the following questions:

- What lives in the river?

- Where does the river go?

- What color is the river?

- How deep is the river?

- How long is the river?

- What is the name of the river?

- Is there anything else you would like to tell me about the river?

Step 9: Allow the child to trace the words in the yellow highlighter with a black pen or pencil.

B.4 Learning Objectives

Math/Science	Language/Literacy	Problem Solving	Motor Skills
•N/A	•Use sentences in conversation to describe, explain or predict outcomes of real or imaginary events. •Initiate and engage in literacy activities. •Write familiar words by looking at the word then copying. •Identify all letters by sight and sound	•Demonstrate Curiosity and ask Questions •Engage in problem solving techniques. •Use words to discuss predictions. •Use language to reiterate process and conclusions •Use language to describe objects by a variety of attributes •Demonstrate understanding of differences between people, animals, plants and other parts of the planet.	•Fine Motor: Use a pen or marker to write familiar words. •Fine Motor: Use a pencil to trace new words

Notes: What did your child do well? Are there any skills they need to continue to work on?

B5. The Oldest Tree - Activity time: 15 minutes

Materials Needed
- ☐ Three (3) Pieces of Paper
- ☐ One (1) Box of Crayons
- ☐ One (1) pen

Instructions:

Step 1: Tell the child that trees live for a very long time. There are some trees alive today that have been around for **hundreds of years**. That is a lot of years.

Step 2: Tell the child to use crayons to draw a picture of a very old tree.

Step 3: Tell the child that you're going to write a story about the life of their tree.

Step 4: Ask the child the following questions about the tree they drew, writing their answers on a piece of paper.

- What year was the tree born?
- Who is its family?
- What things has this tree seen in its' life?
- Who lives in the tree?
- What does the tree eat?
- What does the tree like to do?

Step 5: Ask the child to write their name at the top of the story.

Step 6: Ask the child to write their age on the top of the third piece of paper.

Step 7: Ask the child how old the tree would be if the **tree is the same age as they are.** Help them write that number underneath the number from Step 6.

Step 8: Ask the child how old the tree would be if the tree was **two years older than they are**. Can they add two to their current age? Show them how to count the total number on their fingers. Help them write that number **underneath** the number from Step 7.

Step 9: Ask the child how old the tree would be if the tree was **four years older than they are.** Show them how to count the total number on their fingers. Help them write that number underneath the number from Step 8.

Step 10: Ask the child how old the tree would be if the tree was **zero years older than they are.** Do they know that zero means "none"? Help them write their age underneath the number from Step 9.

Step 11: Continue adding more numbers to their age to see how old the tree could be.

Take it to the next level: Once your child is good at **adding "ages"**, ask your child to find out how old the tree would be if the tree was one year **younger than they are**. Can they subtract by counting on their fingers? Continue with asking the child how old the tree would be by taking away more years

.

B.5 Learning Objectives

Math/Science	Language/Literacy	Problem Solving	Motor Skills
•Solve simple addition and subtraction problems with objects. •Count up to 20 objects, using one to one correspondence. •Recognizes the names of Numerals. •Understands size words (Older, vs. Younger, More vs. Less).	•Write their own name, without help. •Follow three-step directions. •Use sentences in conversation to describe, explain or predict outcomes of real or imaginary events. •Initiate and engage in literacy activities.	•Engage in problem solving techniques. •Use words to discuss predictions •Use language to reiterate process and conclusions •Demonstrate understanding of differences between people, animals, plants and other parts of the planet.	•Fine Motor: Use a pen or marker to write familiar words. •Fine Motor: Use a pencil to trace new words

Notes: What did your child do well? Are there any skills they need to continue to work on?

Gross Motor – Using our large muscles to move!

By Completing Level 3 Activities, We will learn…

- Participate in a variety of gross motor activities that require balance and coordination.
- Hop on one foot five or more times.

Fine Motor – Using our hands to complete tasks

By Completing Level 3 Activities, We will learn…

- Use scissors to cut out an object.
- Use a pen or marker to write familiar words.
- Use a pencil to trace new words.

C1. Re-use Builder - Activity time: 15 minutes

Materials Needed
- ☐ Four(4) empty water bottles or soda bottles
- ☐ Two (2) empty tissue boxes
- ☐ Two (2) empty toilet paper rolls
- ☐ One (1) piece of paper already drawn on
- ☐ One (1) empty milk carton (rinsed out with soapy water)
- ☐ Six (6) plastic straws (optional)
- ☐ One (1) roll of scotch tape

Instructions:

Step 1: Tell the child that people use a lot of stuff. Lots of items are thrown away but most of it can be recycled and **reused for a different purpose**. Today we're going to reuse some items **to build** whatever the child would like.

Step 2: Show the child all of the materials on the materials list. Tell them that everything in front of them had a job, but now their jobs are done. We're going to find a **way to use them in a new way.**

Step 3: Allow the child to build **whatever they like** using the objects presented. They can use tape to hold the items together.

Step 4: Once completed, ask the child the following questions:

- What did you make?
- What can it do?
- What does each part do?
- Can you find other things in the house that can be used a new way?

C.1 Learning Objectives

Math/Science	Language/Literacy	Problem Solving	Motor Skills
•Sort objects into groups by two or more attributes.	•Use sentences in conversation to describe, explain or predict outcomes of real or imaginary events.	•Demonstrate Curiosity and ask Questions •Engage in problem solving techniques. •Use language to reiterate process and conclusions •Use language to describe objects by a variety of attributes	•Gross Motor: balance and coordination.

Notes: What did your child do well? Are there any skills they need to continue to work on?

C2. Pattern Cycle - Activity time: 15 minutes

Materials Needed
- ☐ One (1) roll of painters tape
- ☐ One (1) room large enough for the child to hop on one foot four times on a line.
- ☐ Four (4) different sets of six (6) items which can be recycled (i.e. six empty cereal boxes, six water bottles, six tissue boxes, six empty toilet paper rolls)

Instructions:

Step 1: Have the adult place a **three-foot line of painters tape on the floor**. At one end of the tape, place the items you picked which can be recycled.

Step 2: Tell the child that you're going to **sort the items** in the pile **into four different categories.** Each category will have six items in it.

For Example:
- 6 Empty Cereal Boxes
- 6 Water Bottles
- 6 Tissue Boxes
- 6 Paper Towel Rolls

Step 3: Explain to the child that all of these items can be **recycled** because they are made out of recyclable materials. Items that are recycled are taken to a place where they are made into **something new**. Items that can be recycled are:

- All rinsed cans and tins
- All rinsed plastic bottles
- Cardboard
- Birthday or Christmas cards (without foil or glitter)
- Newspapers, magazines and phone books
- Household paper and envelopes

Step 4: Ask the child create a pattern using all six objects, placing the items at one end of the taped line.

For Example: Can, Can, Cardboard, Water bottle, Can, Can, Cardboard, Water bottle…

Step 5: Tell the child that they are going to move their pattern to the other end of the taped line. Tell them to pick up one item, **hop on one foot** from to **the other end of the line** then **place the item down.**

Step 6: Have the child run back to the pattern and pick up the next item. Have them hop on the taped line to the other end and place that object next to the first object that they had put down. Continue completing the patterns in step 7.

Step 7: Have the child complete at least three different types of patterns using all of the materials. Examples of patterns include:

1. Water bottle, water bottle, tissue box, tissue box, toilet paper roll, toilet paper roll, Cereal box, cereal box, water bottle, water bottle, etc (continue until all 24 items have been used).

2. Water bottle, tissue box, toilet paper roll, cereal box, water bottle, tissue box, toilet paper roll, cereal box (continue until all 24 items have been used).

3. Water bottle, Water bottle, Water bottle, cereal box, cereal box, cereal box, tissue box, tissue box, tissue box, toilet paper roll, toilet paper roll, toilet paper roll, water bottle, water bottle, etc (continue until all 24 objects have been used).

C.2 Learning Objectives

Math/Science	Language/Literacy	Problem Solving	Motor Skills
•Solve simple addition and subtraction problems with objects. •Count up to 20 objects, using one to one correspondence. •Describe shapes by at least two characteristics. •Complete patterns that have two or more elements. •Sort objects into groups by two or more attributes.	•Follow 3-Step Directions	•Engage in problem •Use language to reiterate process and conclusions •Use language to describe objects by a variety of attributes	•Gross Motor: balance and coordination. •Gross Motor: Hop on one foot five or more times.

Notes: What did your child do well? Are there any skills they need to continue to work on?

C3. Recycle Throw - Activity time: 15 minutes

Materials Needed
- ☐ One (1) small trash can
- ☐ Ten (10) Pieces of scratch paper
  (paper that has been written on before)
- ☐ One (1) Roll of painters tape

Instructions:

Step 1: It's time to practice putting items into the recycle bin. Paper is **one item** that can be recycled.

Step 2: The adult should crumple each piece of paper into a small paper ball.

Step 3: Show your child the pieces of paper and say: "This paper is special. They were all in the recycle bin, but they keep hopping out. It your job throw the paper back into the recycling bin until they stop "jumping out"."

Step 4: Tell the child that the small garbage is the recycling can. All of the paper balls need to make it into the recycling can.

Step 5: The adult can decide how far away from the recycling can the child should stand. Once the adult shows the child where to stand allow the child to throw the paper balls into the recycling can.

Step 6: These silly paper balls don't like to stay in the recycling can. The adult can go over to the can and throw the paper balls back out of the can.

Step 7: Have the child continue picking up each paper ball and throwing it back into the garbage can.

Step 8: Wow! What a workout. Keep playing until your child gets tired!

Step 9: Recycling is so very important. Make sure you child places all of the paper balls in the recycling bin at the end of the activity. While he/she is picking each paper ball up, have him/her count the paper balls **to make sure they have all 10!**

C.3 Learning Objectives

Math/Science	Language/Literacy	Problem Solving	Motor Skills
•Count up to 10 objects, using one to one correspondence.	•N/A	•Use language to describe objects by a variety of attributes	•Gross Motor: balance and coordination.

Notes: What did your child do well? Are there any skills they need to continue to work on?

C4. Up, Down, Left and Right - Activity time: 10 minutes

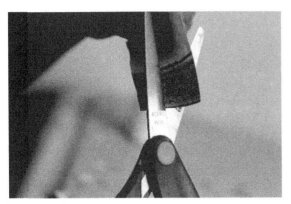

Materials Needed
- ☐ One (1) Pair of child safe scissors
- ☐ One (1) Pen
- ☐ One (1) Piece of Paper

Instructions:

Step 1: The adult should **write the word "start"** on the piece of paper.

Step 2: The adult will make a "word path" using the words : **"right", "left", "up"** and **"down"** on a piece of paper. The words should dictate an "invisible path" (see photo below).

....

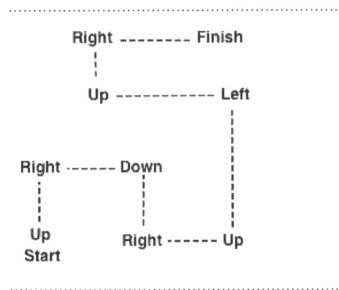

....

Step 2: Allow the child to use child-sized scissors **to cut along the word-path.** Have the child start cutting at the word **"start,"** then follow the directions of the path until they get to **"finish".**

Step 3: Encourage the child to read each **"direction"** word that he/she gets to.

Step 4: Repeat the activity often.

C.4 Learning Objectives

Math/Science	Language/Literacy	Problem Solving	Motor Skills
•N/A	•Follow three-step directions. •Initiate and engage in literacy activities.	•Use language to describe objects by a variety of attributes	•Fine Motor: Use scissors to cut out an object.

Notes: What did your child do well? Are there any skills they need to continue to work on?

C5. Land, Earth and Water - Activity time: 15 minutes

Materials Needed
- ☐ Five (5) Brown pieces of Construction Paper
- ☐ Five (5) Blue pieces of Construction Paper
- ☐ Five (5) Green pieces of Construction Paper
- ☐ One (1) Black Marker
- ☐ A large area where the child can jump around (indoor or outdoor)
- ☐ One (1) roll of painters tape

Instructions:

Step 1: Explain to the child that **each piece of colored paper represents a different part of planet Earth.** The Blue paper represents water, Brown paper represents land and Green paper represents plants/trees.

Step 2: Ask the child to pick a number **(between 1 and 10).** The adult should use a black marker to write that number on each of the brown pieces of paper. That is how many pieces of Land they have on their planet.

Step 3: Ask the child to pick a number **(between 1 and 10)** that's different from the number picked in Step 2. The adult should use a black marker to write that number on the blue pieces of paper. That is how many places of water they have on their planet.

Step 4: Ask the child to pick a number **(between 1 and 10)** that's different from the numbers they have already picked. Write that number on the green pieces of paper. That is how many trees they have on their planet.

Step 5: Tape all of the pieces of paper into the **shape of a large circle on the floor.** The colors should be in **random order.**

Step 6: Have the child step on one piece of paper. Ask them to **say the number that's on that piece of paper**, then "**Hop on 1 Foot" that many times**.

Step 7: Next, have the child step onto the next piece of paper.

Step 8: Repeat steps 6 and 7 until the child has completed the circle.

Step 9: Play the game again and have the child choose **three new numbers** that will correspond to the **colors of the paper.**

C.5 Learning Objectives

Math/Science	Language/Literacy	Problem Solving	Motor Skills
•Count up to 10 objects, using one to one correspondence. •Recognizes the names of Numerals.	•Follow three-step directions.	•Demonstrate understanding of differences between people, animals, plants and other parts of the planet.	•Gross Motor: balance and coordination. •Gross Motor: Hop on one foot five or more times.

Notes: What did your child do well? Are there any skills they need to continue to work on?

Themed Project – Outdoor Exploration

Purpose: To teach the process of finding answers to new questions. Each project guides adults and children through investigating specific questions about the theme. The project starts with the development of a hypothesis that is then tested and researched, concluding with an answer to the hypothesis. Specific Learning Objectives include:

Problem Solving Skills: By Completing Level 3, We will learn…

- o **Predict the results of a familiar action.**
- o **Develop strategies to solve a problem.**
- o **Communicate memories about a sequence of related events that happened in the past.**
- o **Put materials or objects together in new and inventive ways.**
- o **Participate in challenging multi-step activities/projects**
- o **Demonstrate Curiosity and ask Questions.**
- o **Use words to discuss predictions.**
- o **Use language to reiterate process and conclusions.**
- o **Use a variety of techniques to record information and data collection.**

Includes: Activities and discussions that address all areas of academic and developmental skills that meets the Level 3 Learning Objectives. Includes math, science, literacy, art, health/safety, gross motor skills, fine motor skills, music and movement and literacy development.

Order of Operation: These projects are designed to be followed in the order they are laid out, each activity building on the knowledge acquired from previous activities.

Project Objective:

When this project is completed, your child should be able to answer the question:

What is under the dirt?

Introduction Activity:

Step 1: Ask the child to draw a picture of the earth and what lives within.

Step 2: Ask them what they drew and ask them what people and animals live on the earth. Write down exactly what they say on a separate piece of paper.

Step 3: Have your child copy the words with a pen.

Step 4: Make sure to keep this piece of paper on hand to revisit when the project is completed.

Investigation

Section A. What are the layers of the earth?

 Activity #1: How many layers of the earth are there?

Step 1: Ask the child if they know what planet earth is made of.

Step 2: Listen to what they have to say.

Step 3: Ask them if they know what shape the Earth is. What makes the Earth that shape?

 Activity #2 – The Core

Materials Needed
- ½ cup of Ketchup
- One (1) Balloon (not blown up)
- One (1) Plastic spoon

Instructions:

Step 1: Explain to the child that the Earth's core is made of liquid. The liquid is red because it's very hot!

Step 2: Have the child use a spoon to scoop the ketchup into a balloon, filling half of the balloon with ketchup.

Step 3: The adult should tie the balloon closed.

Step 4: This balloon represents the **"Core"** of Planet Earth. The core is very hot.

✎ Activity #3: The Mantle

Materials Needed
- The balloon from activity #1 filled with ketchup (The core)
- One (1) Package of Red Play dough

Instructions:

Step 1: Tell the child:

- The core is liquid and in the middle of the earth.
- Surrounding the core is the Mantle.
- The Mantle is thick and hard. It starts **98,425 feet below** the crust (The crust is where we live). That's really DEEP! The Mantle is about **9,514,436 feet thick.**

Step 2: The child is going to add the Mantle to the Earth's Core (the balloon filled with ketchup from activity #1).

Step 3: Since the Mantel is "hot", we are going to use red play dough to make the Mantle.

Step 4: Have the child cover the **"core"** (balloon from activity #1) with the red play dough "Mantle". Make sure that it's a **thick layer**, since the mantle is **9,514,436 feet thick**.

Step 5: When the child is done, ask them to tell the adult what shape the earth is.

Step 6: Did they form the play dough into **a circle**?   If not, have them reform it.

✎ Activity #4: The Crust

** Start this activity with the following discussion:

Tell the child that animals, humans and everything we see when they go outside **live on the Crust.** The **crust is the dirt** they see when the dig holes in the ground. There is **98,425 feet of Crust** between their feet and the **top of the Earth's Mantle.** The **Crust** is the **thinnest layer** of the Earth.

Materials Needed
- One (1) Piece of Brown Construction Paper
- One (1) Box of Markers
- One (1) Pencil

Instructions:

Step 1: Tell the child that the dirt we walk on is the **outer layer,** the Crust, of the Earth.

Step 2: Have the child use markers to draw pictures of animals and other things they see when they walk outside, on a brown piece of construction paper.

Step 3: Ask the child to use a pencil to **write their name** on the piece of paper.

Step 4: The adult should write the word **"Crust"** on the brown piece of paper with a marker.

Step 5: Encourage the child to trace the word **"Crust"** with the pencil.

Step 6: Help the child wrap the "Crust" (brown piece of paper) around the play dough (the Earth's Mantle) from Activity #3. Use tape to keep it in place.

Section 2. How is dirt made?

> ➤ **Discussion #1: What is dirt?**

Step 1: We just learned about the layers of the earth: The Crust, the Mantle and the Core. Ask the child to describe what the crust looks like to them.

Step 2: Listen to what they have to say.

Step 3: Tell the child that when they play and dig in the dirt, they're actually digging in the Earth's Crust.

Step 4: The Earth's Crust is made up of a variety of materials including: rocks, sand, clay, and organic matter.

> ✏ **Activity #5: How Rocks Are Formed?**

Materials Needed
- One (1) Cup of Room Temperature Water
- Three (3) Drops of red food coloring
- One (1) empty container that can hold one cup of water.
- Access to a freezer
- One (1) plastic spoon

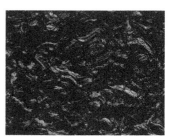

Instructions:

Step 1: Tell the child they are going to discover how **molten rocks** are formed.

Step 2: Molten lava moves from the Earth's core, pushes through the mantle and spurts out of a hole called a **Volcano.**

Step 3: Fill up one cup with **one cup** of "lava" (room temperature water). When filing up the cup, tell the child that **the faucet is pretending to be a Volcano**. The Volcano has erupted and the lava from the Earth's Core is flowing out.

Step 4: Tell the child the **water is warm**, but the real "lava" is very hot.
Step 5: The adult should place three drops of red food coloring in the cup of water (to represent the heat). Allow the child to stir it with a spoon.

Step 6: Tell the child that when lava leaves the Earth's Core it is HOT. It flows through the Mantle and out of the Crust. When it enters the earth's atmosphere, the air is much COOLER.

Step 7: Place the warm water into the freezer (atmosphere) where it's much cooler.

Step 8: Turn a timer on for 30 minutes. Tell the child you are going to check the "lava" when the timer goes off.

Step 8: When the timer goes off (30 minutes later), help the child open the freezer and remove the cup with the red lava.

Step 9: Ask the child to touch the lava. Ask them: "What does it feel like?"

Tell the child that:
- Lava in the earth's core is **liquid** and **very hot.**
- When it flows out of the volcano and reaches a cooler temperature, it gets cold and turn's hard. This is called lava rock (represented by the ice).

✎ **Activity #6: How Is Sand and Clay Formed?**

Materials Needed
- Two (2) large rocks (granite rocks would crumble the most)
- One (1) bucket
- One (1) cup of sand

Instructions:

Step 1: Tell the child they are going to find out how sand is made.

Step 2: When water runs against rocks, the pressure of the water makes rocks rub against each other. This breaks down the rocks, eventually turning them into sand or clay.

Step 3: Tell the child they are going to **pretend that they are the water**. They are going to use pressure to rub the rocks together.

Step 4: Place the two rocks in a bucket.

Step 5: Have the child pick up one rock in each hand, then forcefully rub them together over the bucket. This is called **Erosion.**

Step 6: Help the child rub the rocks together as they **count to 20.**

Step 7: Tell the child to look in the bucket. Do they see any sand or clay?

Step 8: The adult should pour one cup of sand into the bucket.

Step 9: Tell the child that it takes a long time for sand to form.

Step 10: Allow the child to play in the sand and repeat step 7 if desired.

Section 3. The role of Worms in Organic Matter Composting

> ➢ **Discussion #2: What is compost?**

Step 1: Ask the child if they know what happens to a banana peel or a piece of lettuce if left out for **one month.**

Step 2: Listen to what they have to say.

Step 3: Tell them that, over many days, the leftover vegetable and fruit peels turn into compost. The compost breaks down into tiny brown or black components, which looks like dirt.

Step 4: Gardens can grow by using compost as food.

> ✏ **Activity #7: The role of worms in organic composting?**

Materials Needed
- Three (3) to five (5) worms (live fishing worms can be bought in the fishing department of most stores)
- One (1) dark colored plastic container, with a lid.
- One (1) bag of all natural potting soil (no additives)
- One (1) pitcher of water
- Any leftover vegetable or fruit pieces.
- One (1) piece of paper
- One (1) pen

Instructions:

Step 1: Tell the child they are going to find out how important worms are to Planet Earth. Worms eat old food, digest them and make dirt.

Step 2: Show them the worms. If they want to, they can touch them.
    ** Make sure they wash their hands with soap and water when they're through.

Step 3: Have the child help pour the dirt into the dark plastic tub.

Step 4: The adult should add enough water to the dirt to make the dirt moist.

Step 5: Tell the child it's time to **add the worms.** Ask the child to count how many worms there are, while placing each worm into the tub (don't force them to touch the worms if they don't want to).

Step 6: The adult should place the leftover vegetable and fruit pieces into the container, on top of the dirt.

Step 7: Tell the child the worms are going to eat the scraps and make more dirt.

Step 8: Place the lid over the container, leaving at least **one inch uncovered** to allow air into the container.

Step 9: Place the worm bin in a cool, dry place, either indoors or outdoors. **Make sure it's not in the sun.**

Step 10: Have the child make **one tally mark** on a sheet of paper to **signify the day the worm bin was created.**

Step 11: Have the child check the worm box **every** day to see if the food is being eaten or decomposing. Whenever the child checks the worm box, make sure they touch the dirt. The dirt should always feel damp. If it feels as though it is getting dry, add some more water.

Step 12: Every day the child checks the worm bin, **have them make a tally mark on the piece of paper from step 10.** Encourage them to continue making a mark everyday until the food scraps are completely gone.

Step 13: Once the food scraps are gone, ask the child to count how many tally marks they drew. How many days did it take for the worms to eat all of the food scraps?

Optional: Continue taking care of the worm bin, adding more vegetable and fruit scraps. The worms and the dirt can be used to start a garden if desired.

Note: For more information regarding worm bins and other recycling ideas, see the blog titled "Turning Trash into Treasure" at ***jdeducational.com.***

Conclusion

> **Discussion #3: Planet Earth**

Step 1: Review what the child has learned in this project. Ask them what the Earth is made of (Answer: Core, Mantel and Crust).

Step 2: Listen to what they have to say.

Step 3: Next, ask them about each part of the earth. See if they can remember specific attributes about each part of the earth.

Examples:
- The core is hot.
- The mantle is very thick
- The crust is what we walk on.

Step 4: Ask the child how the Crust is made. See if they can remember each component.

Answer:
- Volcanic rock
- Erosion
- Decomposition

Step 5: Is there anything else they learned about Planet Earth?

Memory and Knowledge

After you're finished with this project, ask the child if they want to know anything else about the earth. You may be surprised about their answers! Write them down and encourage them to use books and videos to find out the answers to their questions.

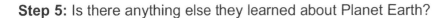

Thanks for playing! See you in the next Unit:
Pre-K Your Way - Level 3, Unit 5
Construction Zone

JDEducational
Play · Learn · Grow

Pre-K YOUR Way

Level 3 Unit 5

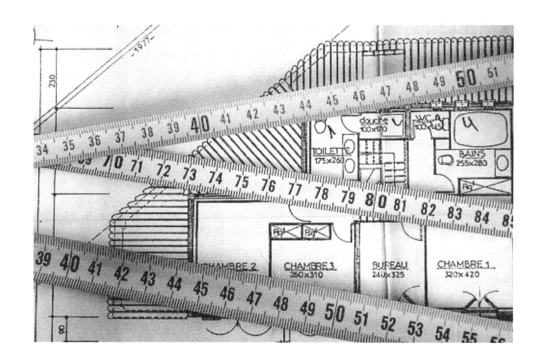

Construction
Building Components and Design Project

Construction Themed Items For Indoor Learning Environment

Now that you have set up your environment, you are ready to place materials in it that directly relate to the theme you are studying! Here are some suggestions of materials your child can free-play with during the "Exploring My Community" Theme:

Books: Age-appropriate books that directly correlate with the monthly theme can be found at your local library or bought separately online. This is a great opportunity to take a trip with your child to your local library and go on a search together. Have them identify words or pictures on the cover of children's books that correlate to the theme. Place a variety of books related to the theme in your child's book area. This will increase opportunities for them to expand their knowledge and use what they learn in the activities to comprehend what they read in the books.

These are age-appropriate books that directly correlate with the monthly theme, which can be found at your local library or bought separately online.

9) Construction– by Sally Sutton and Brian Lovelock

10) Pete the Cat: Construction Destruction – by James Dean

11) The Construction Alphabet Book – by Jerry Pallotta and Rob Bolster

12) Goodnight, Goodnight Construction Site – by Sherri Duskey Rinker and Tom Lichtenheld

13) Where Do Diggers Sleep at Night?– by Brianna Caplan Sayres and Christian Slade

14) Roadwork – by Sally Sutton and Brian Lovelock

15) One Big Building: A Counting Book About Construction (Know Your Numbers) – by

Michael Dahl and Todd Ouren

16) The Construction Crew – by Lynn Meltzer an Carrie Eko-Burgess

Art Area: Encourage your child use this throughout each day by rotating items in an art area. These can be items have already been painted on, paper that they drew on already or leftover materials from another project. Thought provoking art projects are created when children are given unlimited opportunities to explore a variety of materials.

Some suggestions for the art area include:
- Crayons
- Paper
- Pens
- Empty Boxes (all kinds)
- Empty Toilet Paper or Paper Towel Rolls
- Foil
- Clean Q-tips for painting
- Scraps of paper
- Scraps of Yarn
- Scraps of any type of material – including fabric, sand paper, etc.
- Paper Bags
- Straws
- Popsicle Sticks
- Anything else that can be reused.

Suggested Cooking Activities

These are simple cooking and snack-time activities that correlate with the theme. The children can prepare these snacks with adult assistance.

1.   **This Little House:**

Encourage the child to pick three or four different sized graham crackers. They're going to build a house of their choosing. Make sure they remember that there are windows, doors and a roof on a house. How are they going to make those out of their graham crackers? Allow the child to use peanut butter or cream cheese to enable the graham crackers to stick together.

2.   **Popcorn Road:**

Sometimes, when there is construction going on, there are bumps in the middle of the road. These are due to people fixing the street. We're going to make a popcorn road that would be full of bumps we could drive on. Have the child place two long graham crackers next to each other on a plate. Place one Tablespoon of Peanut Butter or Cream Cheese on the top of the plate. Allow the child to dip some pre-popped popcorn into the peanut butter (or cream cheese) and place it onto the graham cracker (road). Now give the child a small, baby carrot and allow them to "drive" the carrot over all of the "bumps in the road".

3.   **Tunnel View:**

To drive through a mountain, cars have to drive through tunnels. Tunnels are very important as they allow cars to get to places they would have not been able to get to because of the mountain or hill that was in the way. Have the child create their own tunnels. Place some sliced deli meats on a paper plate. Have the child roll the meat into a log roll (make sure there is a hole inside so that the cars can go through). Using small crackers or pieces of cheese cut into 1-inch pieces, allow the child to drive the "cars" through the tunnel!

Sensory Bin Suggestions: A sensory bin is a small plastic bucket that is filled with a variety of materials. Sensory bins provide a space to engage in sensory-rich activities that offer opportunities to investigate textures while providing activities for relaxation and self-regulation. Sensory bins encourage language development, small motor development and control, spatial concepts, problem-solving skills and scientific observations. Each month there are suggested sensory bin materials that correlate with the theme of the unit.

Set Up Instructions: In a Plastic Bucket, rotate the following sensory activities throughout the month.

1) Sand Writing Table:

Mix 2 cups of sand, 1 ½ cups cold water and 1 cup of cornstarch together. Stir the mixture for five to ten minutes over medium heat until it becomes thick. Pour the thick sand onto a cookie sheet. After it cools, have your child practice writing the Letter of the Week, Number of the Week and drawing the Shape of the Week in the sand.

Note: You can also use this mixture to build sand castles that will stick together longer.

2) Creations:

Place a variety of paper (recycled, new, small, large, etc.), empty tissue boxes, Empty Toilet Paper rolls, Empty Paper Towel Rolls and unused shoeboxes into the sensory bin. Allow the child to construct and build a variety of different towers and other buildings or creations with the materials. If desired, offer some glue sticks and tape as tools to build.

3) The Construction Zone:

The Construction Zone tends to get dirty at times. Allow the child to put Legos or other plastic blocks, shovels and plastic trucks or tractors into the Sensory bin. Add two Cups full of dirt to the bin. Allow the child to create their own imaginative play scenarios using these items.

4) Clean up Time:

When it's time to rotate toys out of Activity 3 (The Construction Zone), dump the dirt back outside. Keep all of the toys used in the activity in the bucket. Add some dish soap and water to the bucket and some old sponges. Have you child clean the toys so that they are fresh and new, just like how the buildings look after construction is complete.

Dramatic Play Area

This play area allows children to understand and experience the adult world through imitation and creativity. The dramatic play area provides a safe space for young children to create stories while practicing new vocabulary and practicing social skills. It is also a space where groups of children engage in pretend play which provides opportunities to learn self-help skills, share space and materials, take turns and the use abstract thinking. Each month there is a list of suggested materials to integrate into this area, which correlate with the theme of the month.

Suggested props to include in the dramatic play/pretend play area include:

- Large Cardboard Boxes
- Small Shoe Boxes
- Maps of Local Towns
- Tape
- Markers
- Pictures of Different Buildings that have been constructed in different countries
- Cleaned empty containers of all shapes and sizes
- Legos or other blocks
- Paper and Pencils (for drawing plans to build the buildings)
- Swim goggles (to make sure that their eyes are protected)
- Child-sized working gloves
- Child-sized boots

Learning Objectives - Level 3

After completing all modules in the Level 3 Curriculum Series, the child should be able to:

Mathematics
- Solve simple addition and subtractions problems with objects.
- Count up to 20 objects, using one to one correspondence.
- Recognizes the names of Numerals.
- Understands size words (Smaller vs. Larger).
- Describe shapes by at least two characteristics.
- Complete patterns that have two or more elements.
- Sort objects into groups by two or more attributes.
- Show understanding of measurement by using measuring tools.

Science
- Demonstrate Curiosity and ask Questions
- Engage in problem solving techniques.
- Use words to discuss predictions
- Use language to reiterate process and conclusions
- Use a variety of techniques to record information and data collection
- Use language to describe objects by a variety of attributes
- Demonstrate understanding of differences between people, animals, plants and other parts of the planet.
- Complete multi-step projects.

Language and Literacy
- Write their own name, without help.
- Follow three-step directions.
- Use sentences in conversation to describe, explain or predict outcomes of real or imaginary events.
- Initiate and engage in literacy activities.
- Write familiar words by looking at the word then copying.
- Identify all letters by sight and sound

Problem Solving Skills
- Predict the results of a familiar action.
- Develop strategies to solve a problem.
- Communicate memories about a sequence of related events that happened in the past.
- Put materials or objects together in new and inventive ways.
- Participate in challenging multi-step activities.

Gross Motor/Fine Motor Development
- Participate in a variety of gross motor activities that require balance and coordination.
- Hop on one foot five or more times.
- Use scissors to cut out an object.
- Use a pen or marker to write familiar words.
- Use a pencil to trace new words

Part 1: Construction Themed Academic Activities

These activities have been developed to meet specific, age-appropriate, Kindergarten-Readiness skills. These skills are specified in the learning objectives of each activity. The following activities may be completed in any order desired and are specifically designed to address the academic domains: math, science, language, literacy, cognitive, problem solving, and physical development.

Each activity is on its own page. If the adult chooses to print the activities, the space below each activity is provided for adults to write notes regarding the activity. Adults are encouraged to note if the child enjoyed the activity and if the child needs to work on specific learning objectives. Each activity can be repeated more than once to enable the child to master the learning objectives designed for that activity.

A. Math/Science Development

1. Apartments
2. A Colorful City
3. House on Stilts
4. The 10 Most Unique Homes
5. The White House

B. Language/Literacy Development

1. The Construction Day
2. In My House
3. Building Language
4. Architectural Investigation
5. Building Names

C. Physical Development- Gross Motor & Fine-Motor

1. Sandy Beam
2. Orange Cone Weave
3. Safety Search
4. House Jump
5. Washer Road

Mathematical Development – Understanding Numbers and their Purpose

By Completing Level 3 Activities, We will learn how to...

- o Solve simple addition and subtractions problems with objects.
- o Count up to 20 objects, using one to one correspondence.
- o Recognizes the names of Numerals.
- o Understands size words (Smaller vs. Larger).
- o Describe shapes by at least two characteristics.
- o Complete patterns that have two or more elements.
- o Sort objects into groups by two or more attributes.
- o Show understanding of measurement by using measuring tools.

Science/Cognitive Development – Learning How to Solve Problems

By Completing Level 3 Activities, We will learn how to..

- o Demonstrate Curiosity and ask Questions
- o Engage in problem solving techniques.
- o Use words to discuss predictions
- o Use language to reiterate process and conclusions
- o Use a variety of techniques to record information and data collection
- o Use language to describe objects by a variety of attributes
- o Demonstrate understanding of differences between people, animals, plants and other parts of the planet.
- o Complete multi-step projects.

A1. The Apartment - Activity time: 30 minutes

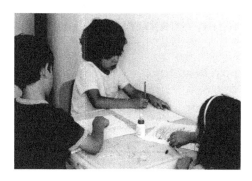

Materials Needed
- ☐ One (1) Piece of Blank White Paper
- ☐ Eighty (72) Toothpicks
- ☐ One (1) Bottle of Elmer's Glue
- ☐ One (1) Set of Markers or Crayons
- ☐ Access to the internet

Instructions:

Step 1: Ask the child to answer the question: "What is an apartment building?"

Step 2: Watch a video of a home or building being built online. An example can be found here:

YouTube Video: 30-Story Building Built In 15 Days (Time Lapse) by: MrBeeblebroxx
https://www.youtube.com/watch?v=rwvmru5JmXk

Step 3: Tell the child that you're going to create an apartment complex for a family to live in. The apartment that this family lives in is on the **10th floor of the building**.

Step 4: Ask the child: "**How many steps** would you need to climb, to get home, if there **are 8 stairs between each floor** of the building?"

Step 5: Have the child use a piece of blank paper and markers to draw **an apartment building that is 10 stories tall.** Help them draw one square or rectangle for each story (**10 squares high).**

Step 6: Help them make a staircase so the people who live on the tenth floor can get to their rooms.

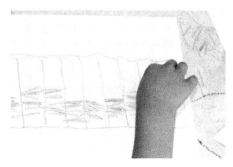

Step 7: Using Elmer's Glue, tell the child to glue **8 toothpicks** inside the first **"floor"** (square/rectangle).

Step 8: Have the child continue to glue eight toothpicks inside each additional level (square or rectangle) until they reach level 10. Make sure they don't put any toothpicks in the top floor (square/rectangle).

Step 9: Ask the child to count the **total number of toothpicks** they glued on the paper (**9 floors x 8 stairs =72 stairs**).

11111111
11111111
11111111
11111111
11111111
11111111
11111111
11111111
11111111

Step 10: Wow! That's a lot of stairs to climb to get to the 10th floor!

A.1 Learning Objectives

Math/Science	Language/Literacy	Problem Solving	Motor Skills
•Solve simple addition and subtraction problems with objects. •Count using one to one correspondence. •Understands size words •Show understanding of measurement by using measuring tools.	•Following Multiple Step Directions	•Demonstrate Curiosity and ask Questions •Engage in problem solving techniques. •Use words to discuss predictions •Use language to reiterate process and conclusions •Use a variety of techniques to record information and data collection •Use language to describe objects by a variety of attributes	•Fine Motor: Use an advanced grasp.

Notes: What did your child do well? Are there any skills they need to continue to work on?

A2. A Colorful City - Activity time: 30 minutes

Materials Needed:
- ☐ One (1) Piece of Blank White Paper
- ☐ One (1) Set of Markers or Crayons
- ☐ One (1) Pen
- ☐ Access to the internet

Instructions:

Step 1: Ask the child: "What is your favorite color?"

Step 2: Take a walk your child around a neighborhood and ask them to point out all of the colors they see (green grass, **yellow flowers, red roofs,** blue doors, etc).

Step 3: Once home, watch a video of different homes. An example is the following YouTube Video:

18 of the Most Colorful Houses Around the World
https://www.youtube.com/watch?v=PAxn5YNCHBw

Step 4: After watching the video of the colorful city homes, ask the child **what color home they would like to have and why.**

Step 5: Using markers or crayons, have the child draw a picture of **the most colorful home** they can think of.

Step 6: When completed, ask the child **what each color represents** (the roof is green, the doors are pink, etc) and **what shape they** are.

Step 7: Ask your child to write their name on their picture.

A.2 Learning Objectives

Math/Science	Language/Literacy	Problem Solving	Motor Skills
•Describe shapes by at least two characteristics. •Complete patterns that have two or more elements. •Sort objects into groups by two or more attributes.	•Use sentences in conversation to describe, explain or predict outcomes of real or imaginary events.	•Demonstrate Curiosity and ask Questions •Use language to describe objects by a variety of attributes.	•Fine Motor: Use a pen or marker to write familiar words. •Fine Motor: Use a pencil to trace new words

Notes: What did your child do well? Are there any skills they need to continue to work on?

A3. The House on Stilts - Activity time: 20 minutes

Materials Needed
☐ One (1) Paper Plate
☐ Fifteen (15) Pretzel Sticks
☐ Five (5) Graham Cracker Squares
☐ Two (2) Tablespoons of Peanut Butter or Cream Cheese
☐ Access to the Internet

Instructions:

Step 1: Explain to the child that sometimes, when a home is built near water, the construction workers build them on stilts to prevent water from entering a home during a flood.

Step 2: Look for some photos on the internet of houses that are on stilts. If you would like, watch the following YouTube video of a house that's built on stilts:

Holiday home on stilts suspended wood structure by OnHome
https://www.youtube.com/watch?v=mMj4-8quEQU

Step 3: Ask the child to think about **how the stilts are placed under the home** and **how they're able to hold the house up.**

Step 4: Next, ask the child: "How much do you think that house weighs?" - Those must be some sturdy pieces of wood to be able to keep the house from falling down.

Step 5: Place one square graham cracker on a plate in front of the child.

Step 6: Place two tablespoons of peanut butter or cream cheese on the plate.

Step 7: Place ten to fifteen pretzel sticks on the plate.

Step 8: Ask the child to build a floor/foundation of stilts (the pretzels) strong enough to hold one square cracker on top. The child can use the peanut butter or the cream cheese as the glue. The pretzel sticks are the stilts and the graham crackers are the floor/foundation of the home.

Step 9: Ask the child if the stilts would be strong enough if he/she added four walls to the home.

Step 10: Have the child **add 4 square graham cracker** "walls" to the house. Use peanut butter or cream cheese as glue.

Step 11: Does the child need to change/modify the stilts in order for them to be strong enough? Go back and watch the video again and see if the child notices how the stilts are placed together to support the house.

Step 12: Add one more cracker as the "roof" to the home. Time to eat!!

A.3 Learning Objectives

Math/Science	Language/Literacy	Problem Solving	Motor Skills
•Count using one to one correspondence.	•Follow directions.	•Demonstrate Curiosity and ask Questions •Engage in problem solving techniques. •Use words to discuss predictions •Use language to reiterate process and conclusions.	•Fine Motor: Grap Motor and Coordination •Fine Motor: Eye-Hand Coordination

Notes: What did your child do well? Are there any skills they need to continue to work on?

A4. Unique Homes - Activity time: 20 minutes

Materials Needed:
- ☐ Seven (7) Sheets of Construction Paper (different colors)
- ☐ One (1) Poster Board
- ☐ One (1) Bottle of Elmer's Glue
- ☐ One (1) Pair of adult sized Scissors
- ☐ One (1) Black Marker
- ☐ Access to the Internet

Instructions:

Step 1: The adult should cut the following shapes out of the construction paper. If your child is able to use child-safe scissors, ask them to help:
- 10 **large** triangles
- 10 **small** triangles
- 8 **large** circles
- 8 **small** circles
- 6 **large** squares
- 6 **small** squares
- 4 diamonds (**any size**)
- 2 ovals (**any size**)

Step 2: Tell the child that homes are built in many different **shapes**, many different **sizes,** many different **areas**.

Step 3: Watch the following YouTube Video: <u>Most unique homes in the world 2014</u> by: <u>Donald Andrew</u>: **https://www.youtube.com/watch?v=9ugJtEgH-ac**

Step 4: After watching the video, ask the child which home was their favorite and why?

Step 5: Ask the child to name all the different shapes that the adult pre-cut.

Step 6: Ask them to identify why each shape is different from the others.

Step 7: Allow the child to create any type of home they would like by gluing the pre-cut shapes onto the large poster board.

Step 8: Once completed, ask the child the following questions:

- Where the doors are
- Where are the windows
- What are all the parts of the house for?

Step 9: The adult should use a black marker to label each part of the home.

A.4 Learning Objectives

Math/Science	Language/Literacy	Problem Solving	Motor Skills
•Count up to 20 objects, using one to one correspondence. •Understands size words. •Describe shapes by at least two characteristics. •Sort objects into groups by two or more attributes.	•Use sentences in conversation to describe, explain or predict outcomes of real or imaginary events.	•Demonstrate Curiosity and ask Questions •Use language to describe objects by a variety of attributes	•Fine Motor: Use scissors to cut out an object.

Notes: What did your child do well? Are there any skills they need to continue to work on?

World Educational Pre-K, Your Way Activity Series. Level 3

253

A5. The White House - Activity time: 30 minutes

Materials Needed
- ☐ One (1) Black Piece of Construction Paper
- ☐ One (1) White Stick of Sidewalk Chalk
- ☐ Ten (10) Small Star Stickers
- ☐ Access to the internet

Instructions:

Step 1: Explain to the child that a very important person lives in the White House. It is the President of the United States. They live in the White House for the entire time they're president. The White House is **very big with lots of rooms** because there are lots of people that work and live there.

Step 2: Look up photos of the White House on the Internet OR look at the White House government site to see a virtual tour of the White House.
https://www.whitehouse.gov/about/inside-white-house/interactive-tour

While looking at the different areas, ask the child what they believe all those rooms are for.

Step 3: Ask the child to use chalk to draw a picture of the White House on a black piece of Construction Paper.

Step 4: Tell the child to place **one star sticker** on ten of their favorite rooms.

Step 5: Tell them that in the White House there are:

- 132 Rooms
- 35 Bathrooms
- 412 Doors
- 147 Windows
- 8 Staircases

Step 6: Walk around your house with the child and count how many there are of the following. Write each number down on a piece of paper.

- Bedrooms
- Bathrooms
- Doors
- Windows
- Staircases

Step 7: After you have written down the number of rooms in your home, compare those numbers to the number of rooms in the White House. Ask the child which house is bigger?

A.5 Learning Objectives

Math/Science	Language/Literacy	Problem Solving	Motor Skills
•Solve simple addition and subtraction problems with objects. •Recognizes the names of Numerals. •Understands size words (Smaller vs. Larger).	•Follow Directions	•Demonstrate Curiosity and ask Questions •Use a variety of techniques to record information and data collection.	•N/A

Notes: What did your child do well? Are there any skills they need to continue to work on?

Language Development – Growing our Vocabulary

By Completing Level 3 Activities, We will learn how to...

- o Follow three-step directions.
- o Use sentences in conversation to describe, explain or predict outcomes of real or imaginary events.
- o Initiate and engage in literacy activities.

Literacy Development – Beginning Reading and Writing

By Completing Level 3 Activities, We will learn how to..

- o Write their own name, without help.
- o Write familiar words by looking at the word then copying.
- o Identify all letters by sight and sound

B1. The Construction Day - Activity time: 15 minutes

Materials Needed
☐ Two (2) Piece of Blank White Paper
☐ One (1) Pen
☐ One (1) Box of Crayons or Markers

Instructions:

Step 1: Sit down with the child and tell them you're going to write a story about building something.

Step 2: The adult should ask the child the following questions and write their responses on a blank piece of paper.

- What should we build today?

- What's the building going to be used for?

- Who's going to use the building – what are their names?

- What are we going to use to make the building?

- What color is the building going to be?

- How tall should this building be?

- Where should we build this building?

- How long is it going to take to build this building?

- What are we going to put inside the building?

- Is there anything else you want to say about the building?

Step 3: Read what you wrote to the child.

Step 4: Tell the child to use crayons to draw a picture of the building they just described on a blank piece of paper.

Step 5: Attach the picture to the story (or answers) from Step 2. Tell the child that this picture is called a building plan.

Step 6: Tell your child to write their name on the "plan". Explain to them that people who create plans are called **architects.** They plan how buildings will be made.

B.1 Learning Objectives

Math/Science	Language/Literacy	Problem Solving	Motor Skills
•N/A	•Write their own name, without help. •Use sentences in conversation to describe, explain or predict outcomes of real or imaginary events. •Initiate and engage in literacy activities.	•Use language to describe objects by a variety of attributes	•Fine Motor: Use a pen or marker to write familiar words. •Fine Motor: Use a pencil to trace new words

Notes: What did your child do well? Are there any skills they need to continue to work on?

B2. In My House - Activity time: 15 minutes

Materials Needed
- ☐ Sale Papers which include pictures of household items (furniture and appliances)
- ☐ One (1) Black Marker
- ☐ One (1) Pair of Child-Safe Scissors
- ☐ One (1) Glue Stick
- ☐ Four (4) Pieces of Paper
- ☐ One (1) Marker
- ☐ One (1) Yellow Highlighter

Instructions:

Step 1: With a yellow highlighter, write the word **Bedroom** on top of one of the blank pieces of paper.

Step 2: With a yellow highlighter, write the word **Bathroom** on top of one of the blank pieces of paper.

Step 3: With a yellow highlighter, write the word **Living Room** on top of one of the blank pieces of paper.

Step 4: With a yellow highlighter, write the word **Kitchen** on top of one of the blank pieces of paper.

Step 5: Tell the child to **find 5 items** in the sale papers that correspond with each word that's written on each piece of paper:

- five items that go in a bedroom
- five for the bathroom
- five for the living room
- five for the kitchen

Step 6: Ask the child to use child **safe scissors to cut 5 items out** for each of the above categories.

Step 7: Encourage them to **sort the pictures into four piles,** each pile corresponding to the rooms of the home written on the white pieces of paper.

Step 8: Tell your child to glue the pictures on the corresponding pieces of paper.
(Example: 5 objects in the living room glued to the piece of paper that says "living room.")

Step 9: When completed, ask the child to name each object. The adult should use a yellow highlighter to write each object's name next to the corresponding picture.

Step 10: Encourage the child to trace all the words with a pen.

B.2 Learning Objectives

Math/Science	Language/Literacy	Problem Solving	Motor Skills
•Solve simple addition and subtraction problems with objects. •Count using one to one correspondence. •Recognizes the names of Numerals. •Sort objects into groups by two or more attributes.	•Write their own name, without help. •Follow three-step directions. •Use sentences in conversation to describe, explain or predict outcomes of real or imaginary events.	•Use language to describe objects by a variety of attributes	•Fine Motor: Use a pen or marker to write familiar words. •Fine Motor: Use a pencil to trace new words

Notes: What did your child do well? Are there any skills they need to continue to work on?

B3. Building Language - Activity time: 25 minutes

Materials Needed
- ☐ One (1) blank piece of white paper
- ☐ One (1) yellow highlighter
- ☐ One (1) Pen or Pencil

Instructions:

Step 1: It's time for a scavenger hunt. Ask the child to walk around the home and point out different areas/parts of the house.

Step 2: The adult should write down what the child points to.

Examples could include:

- Door
- Window
- Wall
- Floor
- Roof
- Carpet

Step 3: Once the child has identified all the parts to the home, have them sit down at a table.

Step 4: Give the child a pen or pencil and have them trace the words written in yellow highlighter. Ask them to identify any of the letters in the words.

B.3 Learning Objectives

Math/Science	Language/Literacy	Problem Solving	Motor Skills
•N/A	•Follow directions. •Use sentences in conversation to describe, explain or predict outcomes of real or imaginary events. •Identify all letters by sight and sound	•N/A	•Fine Motor: Use a pen or marker to write familiar words. •Fine Motor: Use a pencil to trace new words

Notes: What did your child do well? Are there any skills they need to continue to work on?

B4. Architectural Investigation - Activity time: 15 minutes

Materials Needed
- ☐ One (1) Yellow Highlighter
- ☐ One (1) Pen
- ☐ One (1) Piece of blank, white paper
- ☐ One (1) Black Marker

Instructions:

Step 1: Watch the YouTube Video "Top 10 Iconic Buildings in the World":
https://www.youtube.com/watch?v=4mzP7DGmo08

Pause the video at the times listed below and ask the child to identify the **shapes and colors** that are on the building. The adult should write down the names of the shapes and colors with a yellow highlighter.

- 17 Seconds - Dome of the Rock

- 29 Seconds - Christo Redemptor

- 39 Seconds - Big Ben – Pause

- 52 Seconds - Great Wall of China

- 1:11 - Pyramid of Giza

- 1:21 - Petra

- 1:37 - Taj Mahal

- 1:48 and 1:57 - Sydney Opera House

- 2:07 - Statue of Liberty

- 2:28 - Eiffel Tower

Step 2: Encourage the child to use a pen or pencil to trace the shape and color words that the adult has written in yellow highlighter.

B.4 Learning Objectives

Math/Science	Language/Literacy	Problem Solving	Motor Skills
•Describe shapes by at least two characteristics.	•Identify all letters by sight and sound	•Identifying Colors	•Fine Motor: Use a pencil to trace new words

Notes: What did your child do well? Are there any skills they need to continue to work on?

⬉ B5. My Big and Small Name - Activity time: 15 minutes

Materials Needed
- ☐ One (1) Outdoor Environment with Concrete
- ☐ One (1) Piece of Sidewalk Chalk
- ☐ One (1) Small Bucket of Water
- ☐ One (1) Small Paintbrush
- ☐ One (1) Large Paintbrush
- ☐ One (1) Ruler

Instructions:

Step 1: The adult should use sidewalk chalk to write the **child's full name (first and last)** on the floor. Use a ruler to make each letter **one foot tall.**

Step 2: Next, write the child's **full name (first and last)** on a different spot of the sidewalk. Use a ruler to each letter **less than 6 inches tall.**

Step 3: Give the child a small bucket of water and allow them to choose if they would like to use a small paintbrush or large paintbrush to **trace their name.**

Step 4: Have them dip the paintbrush in the water and "paint" their name by tracing the letters. Ask them to name each letter as they trace over it.

Step 5: Ask them: "Where did their name go?" When the water dries, it will be clean.

Step 6: Repeat steps 1 through 5 as many times as you like, making the height of letters different.

B.5 Learning Objectives

Math/Science	Language/Literacy	Problem Solving	Motor Skills
•N/A	•Write their own name, without help. •Identify all letters by sight and sound	•N/A	•Fine Motor: Use a pen or marker to write familiar words. •Fine Motor: Use a pencil to trace new words

Notes: What did your child do well? Are there any skills they need to continue to work on?

Gross Motor – Using our large muscles to move!

By Completing Level 3 Activities, We will learn…

- Participate in a variety of gross motor activities that require balance and coordination.
- Hop on one foot five or more times.

Fine Motor – Using our hands to complete tasks

By Completing Level 3 Activities, We will learn…

- Use scissors to cut out an object.
- Use a pen or marker to write familiar words.
- Use a pencil to trace new words.

C1. Sandy Beam - Activity time: 15 minutes

Materials Needed
- ☐ One (1) five yard Roll of Sand Paper (any type)

Instructions:

Step 1: Tell the child that when construction workers build items made out of wood (like log cabins), the rough edges of the wood need to be sanded so nobody gets splinters when they touch the wood.

Step 2: The adult should create a line with sandpaper on the ground with the rough side up. This line should be at least three feet long.

Step 3: Have the child take their shoes off. Encourage them to walk on the sandpaper in a hcal/tow stepping pattern.

Step 4: Ask the child to count how many steps it takes to get from one end of the sand paper to the other.

Step 5: Can the child take **larger steps** along the sandpaper? Allow them to use their arms for balance, keeping each foot on the sandpaper line.

Step 6: The adult should turn the sand paper over, with the smooth side facing up. Repeat Step 3 through Step 5 with the child moving along the smooth side of the sand paper.

Step 7: Ask the child if they can describe how the "sandpaper" line feels **different.** Is it smooth or rough?

Step 8: Ask the child, "What would they like the wood in their home to be like? **Rough or smooth"?**

Step 9: Are there any other textured items that your child would like to walk on?
(**Examples:** paper, rocks, bark, carpet, tissue paper, ribbon, etc). Ask your child to describe how each item feels.

Note: Sand paper may be a little rough on their skin. If the child doesn't want to walk on the line with bare feet, allow them to try with their socks on or their shoes.

Optional: If the child is having a hard time balancing on the line, allow him/her to jump from one end of the sand paper to the other, counting how many jumps it takes for them to get from one end to the other.

C.1 Learning Objectives

Math/Science	Language/Literacy	Problem Solving	Motor Skills
•Count using one to one correspondence..	•Follow directions.	•Use language to describe objects by a variety of attributes	•Gross Motor: balance and coordination.

Notes: What did your child do well? Are there any skills they need to continue to work on?

C2. Orange Cone Weave - Activity time: 15 minutes

Materials Needed
- ☐ Ten (10) Pieces of Orange Construction Paper
- ☐ Ten (10) Empty Water or Soda Bottles
- ☐ One (1) Timer

Instructions:

Step 1: Roll each orange piece of construction paper into a tube.

Step 2: Place one roll of construction paper into the top of each empty water or soda bottle these are "cones".

Step 3: Place the orange "cones" in a straight line, with two feet in between each bottle.

Step 4: Tell the child that orange cones are used at a construction site to tell people they are working in that area. **Do not go** where construction is happening because it can be **dangerous.**

Step 5: Show the child how to **"weave"** in and out of the "cones" without knocking them over. Do this by running **around** each cone without knocking them down.

Step 6: Encourage the child to mimic what the adult does. Can they do it without knocking the cones over?

Step 7: Now it's time to race! Use the timer to time how fast the child can weave around the cones and get to the other end.

Step 8: Ask the child to repeat the "weaving path" by **jumping** through the cones.

Step 9: Ask the child to repeat the "weaving path" by **hopping** (on one foot) through the cones.

C.2 Learning Objectives

Math/Science	Language/Literacy	Problem Solving	Motor Skills
•N/A	•N/A	•Engage in problem solving techniques. •Use words to discuss predictions •Identify Colors •Understand Visual Representation	•Gross Motor: balance and coordination. •Gross Motor: Hop on one foot five or more times.

Notes: What did your child do well? Are there any skills they need to continue to work on?

C3. Safety Search - Activity time: 15 minutes

Materials Needed

☐ One (1) Home Improvement Store Sale Paper or Magazine
☐ One (1) Piece of Blank, White Paper
☐ One (1) Pair of child-safe scissors
☐ One (1) Glue stick
☐ One (1) Marker (any color)
☐ One (1) Highlighter (any color)

Instructions:

Step 1: Using a Home Improvement magazine or sale paper. Encourage the child to cut the following items out using child-safe scissors:

1. Eyes and Goggles
2. Ears and Ear Plugs/Mufflers
3. Head and Helmet
4. Hands and Gloves
5. Mouth and Breathing Mask/Filter
6. Feet and Sturdy Work Boots

Step 2: Tell them it is very important to stay safe when building and constructing things because the tools can be very dangerous.

Step 3: Use a pen to divide the blank piece of paper into six equal sized areas.

Step 4: Have the child paste the pictures from Step 1 into each box:

Eyes Work Goggles	Ears Ear Plugs	Head Helmet
Hands Gloves	Mouth Mask	Feet Work Boots

Step 5: The adult should use a black marker to write **"Safety First"** at the top of the page.

Step 6: Encourage the child to trace the **"Safety First"** words with a highlighter.

C.3 Learning Objectives

Math/Science	Language/Literacy	Problem Solving	Motor Skills
•N/A	•N/A	•Engage in problem solving techniques. •Use words to discuss predictions •Use language to reiterate process and conclusions •Use language to describe objects by a variety of attributes	•Fine Motor: Use scissors to cut out an object. •Fine Motor: Use a Glue Stick

Notes: What did your child do well? Are there any skills they need to continue to work on?

C4. House Jump - Activity time: 20 minutes

Materials Needed
- ☐ One (1) Roll of Painter's Tape
- ☐ One (1) Outside space or tile floor
- ☐ One (1) Piece of Paper
- ☐ One (1) Pen
- ☐ One (1) Stick of Sidewalk Chalk

Instructions:

Step 1: The adult should draw a plan of their house layout on a blank piece of paper with a pen (Example: see picture):

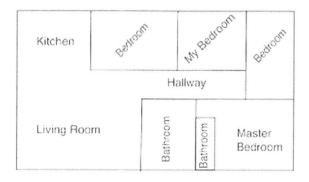

Step 2: With the child, walk around your home and discuss which rooms are **next to** each other.

Step 3: The adult should use a roll of painter's tape, or sidewalk chalk, and the home plan from Step 1, to draw the **same layout** on an outdoor concrete floor.

Step 4: The adult should use sidewalk chalk to **write the name of each room inside of the plan.**

Step 5: The adult should call out the names of the different rooms and encourage the child to hop (on one foot) to that room. Ask the child identify each room by **where the room is located** on the plan.

Example: The Bathroom is **Next to** the Living Room.

Step 6: Continue step 5 until everyone is all hopped out!

C.4 Learning Objectives

Math/Science	Language/Literacy	Problem Solving	Motor Skills
•N/A	•Follow three-step directions.	•Use a variety of techniques to record information and data collection •Use language to describe objects by a variety of attributes	•Gross Motor: balance and coordination. •Gross Motor: Hop on one foot five or more times.

Notes: What did your child do well? Are there any skills they need to continue to work on?

C5. Washer Road - Activity time: 15 minutes

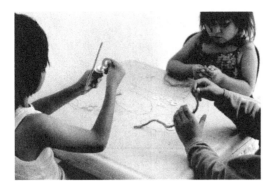

Materials Needed

☐ One (1) Pipe Cleaner
☐ Ten (20) Washers (Hardware): Ten (10) of one size and Ten (10) of another size.

Instructions:

Step 1: Tell the child you are going to be making a **pattern** with the washers.

Step 2: Have the child **separate** the two piles of washers by **size.**

Step 3: Now, tell the child to place the washers onto the pipe cleaner in the following patterns:

- Large washer, Small washer, Large washer, ….

- Large washer, Large washer, Small washer, Small washer, Large washer…

- Small washer, Small washer, Large washer, Large washer, Small washer…

- Small washer, Large washer, Large washer, Small washer, Large washer…

- Can the child or adult come up with any more patterns?

C.5 Learning Objectives

Math/Science	Language/Literacy	Problem Solving	Motor Skills
•Count up to 20 objects, using one to one correspondence. •Complete patterns that have two or more elements. •Sort objects into groups by two or more attributes.	•Follow Directions	•Use language to describe objects by a variety of attributes.	•Fine Motor: Use an advanced grasp

Notes: What did your child do well? Are there any skills they need to continue to work on?

Themed Project – Building Components and Design

Purpose: To teach the process of finding answers to new questions. Each project guides adults and children through investigating specific questions about the theme. The project starts with the development of a hypothesis that is then tested and researched, concluding with an answer to the hypothesis. Specific Learning Objectives include:

Problem Solving Skills: By Completing Level 3, We will learn...

- o **Predict the results of a familiar action.**
- o **Develop strategies to solve a problem.**
- o **Communicate memories about a sequence of related events that happened in the past.**
- o **Put materials or objects together in new and inventive ways.**
- o **Participate in challenging multi-step activities/projects**
- o **Demonstrate Curiosity and ask Questions.**
- o **Use words to discuss predictions.**
- o **Use language to reiterate process and conclusions.**
- o **Use a variety of techniques to record information and data collection.**

Includes: Activities and discussions that address all areas of academic and developmental skills that meets the Level 3 Learning Objectives. Includes math, science, literacy, art, health/safety, gross motor skills, fine motor skills, music and movement and literacy development.

Order of Operation: These projects are designed to be followed in the order they are laid out, each activity building on the knowledge acquired from previous activities.

Project Objective:

When this project is completed, your child should be able to identify all of the different parts of a home and how they come together.

Introduction

Ask the child to draw a picture of the home you live in.

Make sure they have each room identified in their picture and the layout is consistent with the layout of the home they live in.

Investigation

 Activity #1: The Floor/Foundation - Activity time: 30 minutes

Materials Needed
- One (1) Piece of Cardboard (10" x 10")
- One (1) Piece of Plastic Wrap (10" x 10")
- One (1) Piece of Aluminum Foil (10" x 10")
- One (1) Empty Plastic Bowl
- One (1) Package of Markers
- Ten (15) Popsicle Sticks

Instructions:

Step 1: Tell the child you're going to start building a **house today**.

Step 2: Ask the child: "What is the *first part* of building a house?"

Step 3: Explain that in order for walls to stand up, they need to be attached to something. This is called the floor, or **the "foundation"**.

Step 4: Show the child the **three different floor items** (cardboard, foil and plastic wrap). Ask them which one they think would make the better floor? Why?

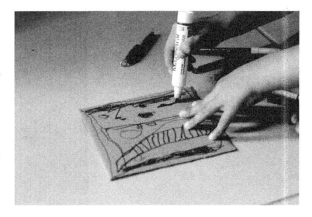

Step 5: It's time to test this theory. **First, place the empty bowl on the table.** Tell the child that you're going to use a bowl to determine if the materials are sturdy enough to build a home on.

Step 6: Place the plastic wrap across the top of the bowl. Have the child place ten popsicle sticks on top of the plastic wrap. What happened? Did it fall down? Ask them if they could build a house on it? Is it strong enough?

Step 7: Next, take the plastic wrap off and place the foil across the top of the bowl. Now have a child place ten popsicle sticks on top of the foil. What happened? Is it strong? Have them place fifteen popsicle sticks on top. Is the foil strong enough to hold all of the popsicle sticks? Would it stay strong enough to hold a house?

Step 8: Next, take the foil off and place the cardboard across the top of the bowl. Now have the child place fifteen popsicle sticks on top of the cardboard. What happened? Ask them to place twenty popsicle sticks on it. Is it strong enough to hold a house?

Step 9: The cardboard would be the best option to build a house on for this project because it is hard, didn't crinkle and the popsicle sticks didn't fall through.

Step 10: Tell the child real buildings are built on solid foundations, such as concrete.

Step 11: Next, allow the child to decorate the floor (cardboard) with the markers. They can draw tile, carpet, hardwood or something else for their home.

Step 12: When finished, put the cardboard in a safe space to be used in Activity #2.

✎ Activity #2: The Walls - Activity time: 30 minutes

Materials Needed
- The "floor" used from Activity #1
- Forty (40) Popsicle Sticks
- One (1) Bottle of Elmer's Glue
- Four (4) Paper Plates

Instructions:

Step 1: Tell the child that this activity is about building the walls of the house. The house is going to be in the shape of a square.

Step 2: Ask the child to describe what a square room would look like (i.e. all equal sides, there are four sides, etc).

Step 3: Show the child forty popsicle sticks. Since there are four sides to a square, we are going to build four "walls" for our house with the popsicle sticks. But the walls must all be the same size.

Step 4: Tell the child to make four equal piles of popsicle sticks, placing one pile on each of the paper plates. Each pile must have the same number of popsicle sticks. Ask the child to place 10 popsicle sticks on each plate.

Step 5: When the child is done sorting, have them count each pile to see if they all have the same number of popsicle sticks. Review with the child that 40 popsicle sticks divided into four equal piles equals 10 popsicle sticks per pile. Allow the child to glue each pile of popsicle sticks together to make four walls. The glue should be placed on the longest edge of the popsicle sticks in order to create a square "wall".

Step 6: With adult support, allow the child to glue each wall of Popsicle sticks together into the shape of a square. Then glue the square onto the cardboard floor.

Step 7: Let walls air-dry overnight.

✎ **Activity #3: Windows -** Activity time: 20 minutes

Materials Needed

- Two (2) Pieces of White Paper
- One (1) Pair of Child Sized Scissors
- One (1) Box of Markers or Crayons
- One (1) Ruler
- One (1) Bottle of Elmer's Glue or Glue Stick
- One (1) Pen

Instructions:

Step 1: Place the dry house from Activity #2 onto a table.

Step 2: Ask the child if they remember what it is. Now ask the child what do they look through when they want to see outside of their home. (Answer: Window)

Step 3: Using a pen and a piece of paper, walk through your home with the child. Ask them to point out all the windows that they see and name what shape they are. Also, ask them if the window is big or small.

Step 4: The adult should write down the characteristics on a piece of paper. (Is the window is big or small and what shape is it?)

Step 5: Walk back to the table where the house project is. Sit down with the child and review the list of windows you discovered were in your home.

Step 6: Tell them windows can be any shape or size. It's time for them to decide how many windows they would like to make for their house and what shape and size they will be. They can be different or the same.

Step 7: Give the child some markers, a ruler and the two pieces of blank, white paper. Allow them to draw all of the windows they would like to put on their house. Have them count how many windows they chose to make.

Step 8: Allow the child to use child-safe scissors to cut out each window.

Step 9: Ask the child to glue them onto the walls of the house with Elmer's Glue or a glue stick.

Step 10: Allow the house-project to dry overnight.

 Activity #4: Doors/Entrance and Exit - Activity time: 20 minutes

Materials Needed
- Two (2) Pieces of Construction paper (any color)
- One (1) Black marker
- One (1) Bottle of Elmer's Glue
- One (1) Pair of child-safe Scissors
- One (1) Package of ½ inch or ¼ inch Craft Pom-Pom balls

Instructions:

Step 1: Place the house-project from activity #3 onto the table. Today we're going to investigate doors.

Step 2: Encourage the child to walk through your house and find all the doors.

Step 3: Ask them if the doors are different, or all the same? Are there sliding doors, doors on hinges, screen doors, closet doors, etc? If the child notices there are different doors in their home, ask them what makes them different?

Step 4: Now that the child has investigated the doors in your home, have them sit at the table. Tell them they're going to be able to draw doors for their house-project.

Step 5: Give the child construction paper and crayons or markers. Allow them to draw all of the doors they want in their home.

Step 6: Ask them what shapes the doors are, and what they're for.

Step 7: Tell the child to use child-safe scissors to cut the doors out.

Step 8: Ask the child the following questions:

1. How do they open the door?
2. What do they hold onto to make it open? (Answer: Doorknobs)
3. Where are the doorknobs placed?
4. Are they in the middle of the door or on the side of the door?
5. Can anyone reach the doorknobs in your house?
6. Why do they think the doorknobs are put in that spot?

Step 9: Show them the craft Pom-Pom craft balls and tell them they can use those for the doorknobs. Allow the child to pick out the amount of "door knobs" they will need for their home and glue them onto each door.

Step 10: Allow the child to glue the doors onto the house-project.

Step 11: Place the house-project away to dry overnight.

 Activity #5: Roofs and their Purpose - Activity time: 30 minutes

Materials Needed
- Three (3) Square Pieces of Cardboard (10 inches by 10 inches)
- One (1) Square Piece of Foil (10 inches by 10 inches)
- One (1) Roll of Scotch Tape
- One (1) Paper Towel Square
- One (1) Kitchen spoon
- One (1) Paper Cup

Instructions:

Step 1: Place the house-project from activity #4 onto the table. Today we're going to discuss the roof and its importance when building a shelter or home.

Step 2: If possible, take the child outside and have them look at the roof. What is it? Ask them why it's there.

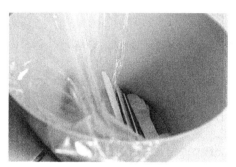

Step 3: Go back inside. Sit down next to the house they built. Explain to them that the roof has a lot of responsibilities; it keeps the weather and all the elements out of buildings. Roofs help keep the rain from coming in the house, it helps give shade during the summer and stops the wind from blowing inside the house. Roofs are very important.

Step 4: Tell the child that it's time to make a roof for their house.

Step 5: Ask the child if they know what shape roofs are. Some are flat and some are triangles.

Step 6: Ask the child if they know why most roofs are in the shape of a triangle? Tell them that they are in the shape of a triangle so that when it rains, the water runs off of the roof and onto the ground. If the roof did not have an angel, then the water wouldn't fall to the ground and might leak into the house.

Step 7: It's important that the roof we make for the house-project doesn't allow water into the house.

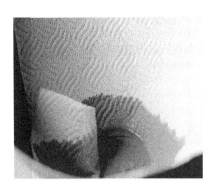

Step 8: Place a piece of foil onto the table. Place a cup of water and a plastic spoon next to the foil. Ask the child to place three spoons full of water onto the foil. What happened? Did the water stay on top of the foil or did it go through it?

Step 9: Place a paper towel onto the table. Place a cup of water and a plastic spoon next to the paper towel. Ask the child to place three tablespoons full of water onto the paper towel. What happened? Did the water stay on top of the paper towel or did it go through it?

Step 10: Which material would be better used to keep water out of their house? That's right, the foil because it keeps water out.

Step 11: Now we have to make sure the roof is sturdy because we don't want the wind to blow it away.

Step 12: Have the adult bend one of the pieces of cardboard (10 inch by 10 inch) in half, and then open it up again. The crease in the middle creates two angles, like the top of a triangle.

Step 13: With adult support, allow the child to tape the creased cardboard piece (from Step 12) onto a flat piece of cardboard (which will act as the base of the triangle) in order to form a triangle shape.

Step 14: The adult should cut off the extra part of the flat cardboard that is longer than the triangle.

Step 15: Use tape to attach the foil to the top of the triangle to add "protection" from the rain.

See Picture:

Step 16: Use tape or glue to attach the triangle roof to the top of the house.

Step 17: Cover up any holes in the roof by adding more foil.

Step 18: The house-project is complete!

Step 19: Take a walk around your neighborhood, looking at all the homes. Ask your child to describe the similarities and differences of each home

Conclusion: Memory and Knowledge

Now ask the child to identify all the areas of the home they created. If possible, drive past a construction site in your area and see if the child can identify what part of the building the construction workers are working on that day.

....

Thanks for playing! See you in the next Unit:
Pre-K Your Way - Level 3, Unit 6
Oceanography - The Five Oceans and What Lives Within

JDEducational
Play • Learn • Grow

Pre-K YOUR Way
Level 3 Unit 6

Oceanography
Ocean Discovery Project

Ocean Themed Items For Indoor Learning Environment

Now that you have set up your environment, you are ready to place materials in it that directly relate to the theme you are studying! Here are some suggestions of materials your child can free-play with during the "Exploring My Community" Theme:

Books: Age-appropriate books that directly correlate with the monthly theme can be found at your local library or bought separately online. This is a great opportunity to take a trip with your child to your local library and go on a search together. Have them identify words or pictures on the cover of children's books that correlate to the theme. Place a variety of books related to the theme in your child's book area. This will increase opportunities for them to expand their knowledge and use what they learn in the activities to comprehend what they read in the books.

These are age-appropriate books that directly correlate with the monthly theme, which can be found at your local library or bought separately online.

1. The Rainbow Fish – by Marcus Pfister and J Alison James

2. Wish for a Fish: All About Sea Creatures – by Bonnie Worth

3. What If There Were No Sea Otters?: A Book About the Ocean Ecosystem (Food Chain Reactions) – by Suzanne Slade and Carol Schwartz

4. Froggy Learns to Swim – by Jonathon London and Frank Remkiewiez

5. Commotion in the Ocean – by Giles Andreae and David Woitowycz

6. I'm the Biggest Thing in the Ocean! – by Kevin Sherry

Art Area: Encourage your child use this throughout each day by rotating items in an art area. These can be items have already been painted on, paper that they drew on already or leftover materials from another project. Thought provoking art projects are created when children are given unlimited opportunities to explore a variety of materials.

Some suggestions for the art area include:
- Crayons
- Paper
- Pens
- Empty Boxes (all kinds)
- Empty Toilet Paper or Paper Towel Rolls
- Foil
- Clean Q-tips for painting
- Scraps of paper
- Scraps of Yarn
- Scraps of any type of material – including fabric, sand paper, etc.
- Paper Bags
- Straws
- Popsicle Sticks
- Anything else that can be reused.

Suggested Cooking Activities

These are simple cooking and snack-time activities that correlate with the theme. The children can prepare these snacks with adult assistance.

1.   **Sand Pudding:**

Make Vanilla Instant Pudding and spoon into cups. Sprinkle a top layer of cracker crumbs on the top of the cup.

2.   **Blue Ocean:**

Empty a package of blue Kool-Aid into a pitcher. Have the child say, "Let the Tide Roll In" and add water to the pitcher. Wow! It turns ocean blue magically!

3.   **Crab-in Around:**

Cut a piece of bread into squares. Square crackers could be used as a substitute for the bread. Ask the child to make some pincher feet with pretzel sticks, placing the feet on each side of the cracker. See Diagram Below:

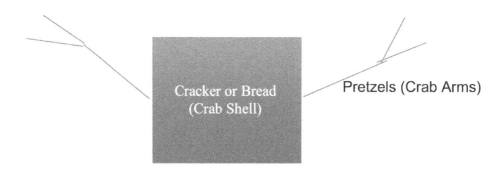

Cracker or Bread
(Crab Shell)

Pretzels (Crab Arms)

Sensory Bin Suggestions: A sensory bin is a small plastic bucket that is filled with a variety of materials. Sensory bins provide a space to engage in sensory-rich activities that offer opportunities to investigate textures while providing activities for relaxation and self-regulation. Sensory bins encourage language development, small motor development and control, spatial concepts, problem-solving skills and scientific observations. Each month there are suggested sensory bin materials that correlate with the theme of the unit.

Set Up Instructions: In a Plastic Bucket, rotate the following sensory activities throughout the month.

1.   **Sand Writing Table:**

Mix 2 cups of sand, 1 ½ cups cold water and 1 cup of cornstarch together. Stir the mixture for five to ten minutes over medium heat until it becomes thick. Pour the thick sand onto a cookie sheet. After it cools, have your child practice writing the Letter of the Week, Number of the Week and drawing the Shape of the Week in the sand.

Note: You can also use this mixture to build sand castles that will stick together longer.

2.   **Blue Water:**

Place water mixed with blue food coloring into the sensory bin. Add plastic Sea Animals to encourage pretend play.

3.   **Salt Tray:**

Put two cups of salt into a sensory bin. Add plastic spoons and paper cups for scooping and pouring practice.

Dramatic Play Area

This play area allows children to understand and experience the adult world through imitation and creativity. The dramatic play area provides a safe space for young children to create stories while practicing new vocabulary and practicing social skills. It is also a space where groups of children engage in pretend play which provides opportunities to learn self-help skills, share space and materials, take turns and the use abstract thinking. Each month there is a list of suggested materials to integrate into this area, which correlate with the theme of the month.

Suggested props to include in the dramatic play/pretend play area include:

- Blanket/Towel
- Sunglasses
- Flip-Flops
- Radio,
- Swim suit
- Beach ball
- Ice chest
- Pictures of the Beach
- Buckets/Pails/Sand Shovels/Sand tools/Sand Molds
- Beach chairs
- Umbrellas
- Empty suntan lotion bottles (washed out with soap and water)
- Books about the Beach
- Pictures of kids playing at the beach
- A paper sun on the wall (for decoration)
- Music with ocean sounds or music about the beach
- Beach bags
- Swimming fins
- Snorkeling gear
- Beach hats and visors
- Sea shells
- Plastic fish
- An empty outdoor wading pool

Learning Objectives - Level 3

After completing all modules in the Level 3 Curriculum Series, the child should be able to:

Mathematics
- Solve simple addition and subtractions problems with objects.
- Count up to 20 objects, using one to one correspondence.
- Recognizes the names of Numerals.
- Understands size words (Smaller vs. Larger).
- Describe shapes by at least two characteristics.
- Complete patterns that have two or more elements.
- Sort objects into groups by two or more attributes.
- Show understanding of measurement by using measuring tools.

Science
- Demonstrate Curiosity and ask Questions
- Engage in problem solving techniques.
- Use words to discuss predictions
- Use language to reiterate process and conclusions
- Use a variety of techniques to record information and data collection
- Use language to describe objects by a variety of attributes
- Demonstrate understanding of differences between people, animals, plants and other parts of the planet.
- Complete multi-step projects.

Language and Literacy
- Write their own name, without help.
- Follow three-step directions.
- Use sentences in conversation to describe, explain or predict outcomes of real or imaginary events.
- Initiate and engage in literacy activities.
- Write familiar words by looking at the word then copying.
- Identify all letters by sight and sound

Problem Solving Skills
- Predict the results of a familiar action.
- Develop strategies to solve a problem.
- Communicate memories about a sequence of related events that happened in the past.
- Put materials or objects together in new and inventive ways.
- Participate in challenging multi-step activities.

Gross Motor/Fine Motor Development
- Participate in a variety of gross motor activities that require balance and coordination.
- Hop on one foot five or more times.
- Use scissors to cut out an object.
- Use a pen or marker to write familiar words.
- Use a pencil to trace new words

Part 1: Ocean Themed Academic Activities

These activities have been developed to meet specific, age-appropriate, Kindergarten-Readiness skills. These skills are specified in the learning objectives of each activity. The following activities may be completed in any order desired and are specifically designed to address the academic domains: math, science, language, literacy, cognitive, problem solving, and physical development.

Each activity is on its own page. If the adult chooses to print the activities, the space below each activity is provided for adults to write notes regarding the activity. Adults are encouraged to note if the child enjoyed the activity and if the child needs to work on specific learning objectives. Each activity can be repeated more than once to enable the child to master the learning objectives designed for that activity.

A. Math/Science Development

1. Why do boats float in the Ocean?
2. Ocean Patterning
3. Smooth Vs. Rough
4. Sea Shell Counting
5. Edible Aquarium

B. Language/Literacy Development

1. In the Ocean
2. Salt Painting
3. Shell Homes
4. Five Oceans
5. Sandy Name

C. Physical Development- Gross Motor & Fine-Motor

1. Sensory Beach
2. Sounds of the Sea
3. Snorkeling
4. How Big am I?
5. Dolphin Dance

Mathematical Development – Understanding Numbers and their Purpose

By Completing Level 3 Activities, We will learn how to…

- o Solve simple addition and subtractions problems with objects.
- o Count up to 20 objects, using one to one correspondence.
- o Recognizes the names of Numerals.
- o Understands size words (Smaller vs. Larger).
- o Describe shapes by at least two characteristics.
- o Complete patterns that have two or more elements.
- o Sort objects into groups by two or more attributes.
- o Show understanding of measurement by using measuring tools.

Science/Cognitive Development – Learning How to Solve Problems

By Completing Level 3 Activities, We will learn how to..

- o Demonstrate Curiosity and ask Questions
- o Engage in problem solving techniques.
- o Use words to discuss predictions
- o Use language to reiterate process and conclusions
- o Use a variety of techniques to record information and data collection
- o Use language to describe objects by a variety of attributes
- o Demonstrate understanding of differences between people, animals, plants and other parts of the planet.
- o Complete multi-step projects.

A1. Why do boats float in the ocean? Activity time: 15 minutes

Materials Needed
- ☐ Two (2) Large Bowls filled with water
- ☐ One Half (1/2) Cup of Salt
- ☐ Two (2) Eggs

Instructions:

Step 1: Have the child fill two bowls, each with **two cups** of water.

Step 2: Add 1/2 cup of salt to one of the bowls of water. Mix until the salt is dissolved.

Step 3: Ask the child: "Where is the salt? Can you see it? Why did it dissapear?"

Step 4: Ask the child what they think will happen if you add an egg to the water.

Step 5: Allow the child to place one egg into each bowl.

Step 6: Discuss what happened.

Step 7: Ask the child: "Why does one egg sink and the other egg float?"

> **Answer:**
> Dissolved salt adds **to the mass of the water** and makes **the water become denser.** Because objects float better on a dense surface, **the egg floats better in salt water** rather than fresh water.

Step 8: Tell the child that Ocean water has salt in it! Ask the child: "What types of objects float in the Ocean?"

A.1 Learning Objectives

Math/Science	Language/Literacy	Problem Solving	Motor Skills
•Describe objects by characteristics.	•Follow three-step directions. •Use sentences in conversation to describe, explain or predict outcomes of real or imaginary events.	•Demonstrate Curiosity and ask Questions •Engage in problem solving techniques. •Use words to discuss predictions •Use language to reiterate process and conclusions •Use language to describe objects by a variety of attributes.	•N/A

Notes: What did your child do well? Are there any skills they need to continue to work on?

A2. Ocean Patterns Activity time: 25 minutes

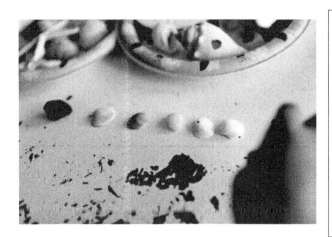

Materials Needed
- ☐ One (1) Empty plastic bottle (an empty two-liter soda bottle, water bottle, juice bottle, etc. would work great)
- ☐ One (1) Cup of small rocks
- ☐ One (1) Cup of Sand
- ☐ One (1) Cup of Small Seashells (that can fit inside the top of an empty bottle)
- ☐ One (1) Cup of Water
- ☐ Three (3) Paper Plates

Instructions:

Step 1: Have the child place the rocks on one paper plate, the sand on another paper plate and the seashells on another paper plate.

Step 2: Give the child the empty plastic bottle and tell them that you are going to find out how sand is made.

Step 3: Have the child put a **half-inch** layer of **rocks** into the plastic bottle.

Step 4: Have the child put a **half-inch** layer of **sand** into the plastic bottle.

Step 5: Have the child put a **half-inch** layer of **seashells** into the plastic bottle.

Step 6: Repeat steps 2 through 4, creating a three-part pattern, until all of the items are in the bottle.

Step 7: Tell the child that the most common natural process of sand formation is called **weathering**. The majority of sand comes from the wearing down of the rocks by the force of the waves smashing up against the shells and the rocks. Eventually all of the rocks become small and turn into sand.

Step 8: Have the child add one cup of water to the bottle and put the top on.

Step 9: Encourage the child to shake the bottle. Explain that the child is the force behind the waves slamming up against the seashore. Eventually the rocks and the seashells in the bottle will turn into sand, although it will take a long time!

A.2 Learning Objectives

Math/Science	Language/Literacy	Problem Solving	Motor Skills
•Complete patterns that have two or more elements. •Sort objects into groups by two or more attributes.	•Follow three-step directions. •Use sentences in conversation to describe, explain or predict outcomes of real or imaginary events.	•Demonstrate Curiosity and ask Questions •Engage in problem solving techniques. •Use words to discuss predictions •Use language to reiterate process and conclusions •Use language to describe objects by a variety of attributes	•Fine Motor: Placing small objects into a container.

Notes: What did your child do well? Are there any skills they need to continue to work on?

A3. Smooth vs. Rough Activity time: 20 minutes

Materials Needed

- ☐ Collection of variety of seashells and small rocks
- ☐ Two (2) empty plates or bowls
- ☐ One (1) Clean Sock

Instructions:

Step 1: Mix all of the seashells and rocks together into a pile and place them into a clean sock.

Step 2: Have the child put their hand into the sock, touching the shells and the rocks.

Step 3: Ask them: "What are you touching? What does it feel like? Is it smooth or rough"

Step 4: Can they guess what is in the sock?

Step 5: Direct them to take each item out (one by one) and place the **rough items** into one bowl and the **smooth items** in another.

Step 6: Ask your child to sort the shells by **shape.**

Step 7: Ask your child to sort the shells by **size.**

Step 8: Ask your child to make the following patterns with the shells and rocks:

A. Rock, Shell, Rock, Shell ……

B. Rock, Rock, Shell, Rock, Rock, Shell….

C. Shell, Shell, Rock, Rock, Shell, Rock, Shell, Shell, Rock, Rock, Shell, Rock…

A.3 Learning Objectives

Math/Science	Language/Literacy	Problem Solving	Motor Skills
•Understands size words (Smaller vs. Larger). •Describe shapes by at least two characteristics. •Complete patterns that have two or more elements. •Sort objects into groups by two or more attributes.	•Follow three-step directions. •Use sentences in conversation to describe, explain or predict outcomes of real or imaginary events.	•Demonstrate Curiosity and ask Questions •Use words to discuss predictions •Use language to reiterate process and conclusions •Use language to describe objects by a variety of attributes	•N/A

Notes: What did your child do well? Are there any skills they need to continue to work on?

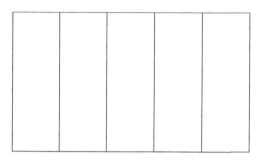

A4. Sea Shell Counting Activity time: 15 minutes

Materials Needed
- ☐ Five (5) Sea Shells
- ☐ Two (2) Water based finger-paint colors
- ☐ One (1) Marker
- ☐ One (1) Piece of Blank Paper
- ☐ One (1) Paper Plate
- ☐ One (1) Pen

Instructions:

Step 1: Divide two pieces of paper into five columns by drawing four vertical lines on each piece of paper. Each line should be the same width apart.

Step 2: On one piece of paper, the adult should use a pen to write the following numbers on the top of each column: 1 in the first column, 2 in the second column, 3 in the third column, 4 in the fourth column and 5 in the fifth column.

First Piece of Paper

1	2	3	4	5

Step 3: On the second piece of paper, the adult should use a pen to write the following numbers on the top of each column: 6 in the first column, 7 in the second column, 8 in the third column, 9 in the fourth column and 10 in the fifth column.

Second Piece of Paper

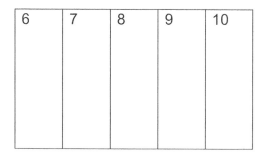

6	7	8	9	10

Step 4: Have the child trace each number with a marker of their choosing.

Step 5: Put two tablespoons of the water-based finger-paint onto a paper plate.

Step 6: Ask the child to pick out a seashell, dip it into the paint and put the seashell onto the first column of the paper, under the number 1.

Step 7: Have the child lift up the seashell and see the seashell print that was left behind. Count "one" seashell (under the number one).

Step 8: Have the child continue making seashell prints, the total number which corresponds with the numbers written at the top of the column (two seashell prints in the "2" column, three seashell prints in the "3" column, etc).

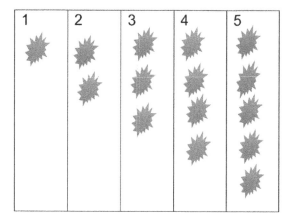

Step 9: Ask the child to count the **total amount of seashells under each column**, reminding them that the amount of seashell prints match the number that is written on top of each column.

Step 10: Tell the child to **add the following number to seashell prints together**:

- Add the total amount of seashells in the **first row** of the **first piece of paper** and/plus the **first row** of the **second piece** of paper (Answer: 1 sea shell + 5 sea shells = 6 sea shells).

- Add the total amount of seashells in the **second row** of the **first piece of paper** and the **second row** of the **second piece of paper** (Answer: 2 sea shell + 6 sea shells = 8 sea shells).

- Add the total amount of seashells in the **third row** of the **first piece of paper** and the **third row** of the **second piece of paper** (Answer: 3 sea shell + 8 sea shells = 11 sea shells).

- Add the total amount of seashells in **fourth row** of the **first piece of paper** and the **fourth row** of the **second piece of paper** (Answer: 4 sea shell + 9 sea shells = 13 sea shells).

- Add the total amount of seashells in the **fifth row** of the **first piece of paper** and the **fifth row** of the **second piece of paper** (Answer: 5 sea shell + 10 sea shells = 15 sea shells).

Step 11: Ask the child to add more columns together by describing the columns by **ordinal numbers** (first, second, third….. etc). Do they remember learning about **Ordinal Numbers** in the Transportation theme?

A.4 Learning Objectives

Math/Science	Language/Literacy	Problem Solving	Motor Skills
•Solve simple addition and subtractions problems with objects. •Count up to 20 objects, using one to one correspondence. •Recognizes the names of Numerals. •Understands size words (More vs. Less). •Show understanding of measurement by using measuring tools.	•Follow three-step directions. •Use sentences in conversation to describe, explain or predict outcomes of real or imaginary events.	•Demonstrate Curiosity and ask Questions •Engage in problem solving techniques. •Use words to discuss predictions •Use language to reiterate process and conclusions •Use a variety of techniques to record information and data collection	•Fine Motor: Use a pen or marker to write familiar words or numbers.

Notes: What did your child do well? Are there any skills they need to continue to work on?

A5. Edible Aquarium Activity time: 20 minutes

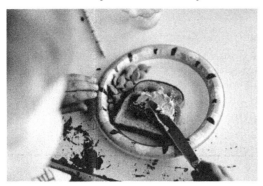

Materials Needed
☐ Two (2) Tablespoons of Cream Cheese ☐ Two (2) Drops of Blue Food Coloring ☐ One (1) Piece of Toast (or Bread) ☐ Ten (10) Goldfish Crackers

Instructions:

Step 1: The adult should prepare toast in the toaster (optional).

Step 2: The child can help the adult add one or two drops of blue food coloring to two tablespoons of cream cheese and stir.

Step 3: Allow the child to use a **plastic knife** to spread the blue cream cheese onto the toast.

Step 4: Have the child place **10 goldfish crackers** onto the toast, counting cach fisth.

Step 5: Have the child eat **one goldfish**.

Step 6: Ask them to count, one by one, how many goldfish are left.

Step 7: Have the child repeat the following phrase:

"10 goldfish **minus** 1 goldfish **equals** 9 goldfish."

Step 8: Repeat Step five until all goldfish are complete.

Step 9: Repeat Steps 1 through 6, giving the child the following directions:

- Place ten goldfish on the piece of toast and **eat two**. Ask the child how many goldfish are left. (Answer: 10-2 = 8 goldfish). Ask the child to repeat Step 8, eating two goldfish each time, counting to total left each time.

- Place ten goldfish on the piece of toast and **eat three**. Ask the child how many goldfish are left. (Answer: 10-3 = 7 goldfish). Ask the child to repeat Step 8, eating three goldfish each time, counting to total left each time.

- Place ten goldfish on the piece of toast and **eat four**. Ask the child how many goldfish are left. (Answer: 10-4 = 6 goldfish). Ask the child to repeat Step 8, eating four goldfish each time, counting to total left each time.

- Place ten goldfish on the piece of toast and **eat five**. Ask the child how many goldfish are left. (Answer: 10-5 = 5 goldfish). Ask the child to repeat Step 8, eating five goldfish each time, counting to total left each time.

Step 10: Now it's time to eat the toast!

A.5 Learning Objectives

Math/Science	Language/Literacy	Problem Solving	Motor Skills
•Solve simple addition and subtractions problems with objects. •Count up to 10 objects, using one to one correspondence. •Recognizes the names of Numerals. •Understands size words (More vs. Less).	•Follow three-step directions. •Use sentences in conversation to describe, explain or predict outcomes of real or imaginary events.	•Engage in problem solving techniques. •Use language to reiterate process and conclusions	•Fine Motor: Using utensils appropriately

Notes: What did your child do well? Are there any skills they need to continue to work on?

Language Development – Growing our Vocabulary

By Completing Level 3 Activities, We will learn how to…

- Follow three-step directions.
- Use sentences in conversation to describe, explain or predict outcomes of real or imaginary events.
- Initiate and engage in literacy activities.

Literacy Development – Beginning Reading and Writing

By Completing Level 3 Activities, We will learn how to..

- Write their own name, without help.
- Write familiar words by looking at the word then copying.
- Identify all letters by sight and sound

B1: In the Ocean Activity time: 20 minutes

Materials Needed
☐ One (1) Piece of Blue Construction Paper ☐ One (1) Marker ☐ One (1) Pack of Crayons/Markers/Colored Pencils ☐ Computer or Tablet With Internet Access

Instructions:

Step 1: Using a computer or other electronic device, watch a video of animal **that live under the ocean.** A great example is the Trailer to Disney Nature's Movie: "Exploring Oceans" (3 minutes long). You can leave the sound on or off: https://www.youtube.com/watch?v=x8VxozQuG2o

Step 2: Fold a piece of blue construction paper in half. Open it back up and use a black marker to draw a line across the fold.

Sky
Ocean

Step 3: Explain to the child that on this piece of paper, the **Ocean will be represented below the line** and the **Sky will be represented above the line.** Ask the child what they remember from the video and discuss all of the different animals.

Step 4: Have the child use crayons to draw what lives in the ocean and what lives in the sky on the piece of paper. The Ocean animals go **below the line** and the Sky animals go **above the line.**

Step 5: Ask the child what the animals are doing and write down the story they describe.

Step 6: Ask your child to write their name on the top of their story.

B.1 Learning Objectives

Math/Science	Language/Literacy	Problem Solving	Motor Skills
•Sort objects into groups.	•Write their own name, without help. •Use sentences in conversation to describe, explain or predict outcomes of real or imaginary events.	•Demonstrate Curiosity and ask Questions •Use words to discuss predictions •Use language to reiterate process and conclusions •Use language to describe objects by a variety of attributes •Demonstrate understanding of differences between people, animals, plants and other parts of the planet.	•Fine Motor: Use a pen or marker to write familiar words. •Fine Motor: Use a pencil to trace new words

Notes: What did your child do well? Are there any skills they need to continue to work on?

B.2. Salt Painting Activity time: 20 minutes

Materials Needed

☐ Three (3) to Five (5) plastic Ziploc baggies
☐ One (1) Cup Salt
☐ Three (3) to Five (5) different food coloring packets
☐ One (1) Bottle of Elmer's Glue
☐ One (1) Piece of White Construction Paper

Instructions:

Step 1: Place 2 tablespoons of salt into each plastic baggie.

Step 2: Add 3 drops of food coloring to each plastic baggie, putting a different color in each bag.

Step 3: Holding the bag shut, shake the baggies and lay to dry for five minutes.

Step 4: Open the two baggies and allow the child to touch the salt.

Step 5: Ask the child what the salt feels like.

Step 6: Ask the child what the salt smells like.

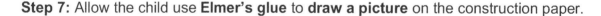

Step 7: Allow the child use **Elmer's glue** to **draw a picture** on the construction paper.

Step 8: Ask the child to sprinkle the paper with the different colors of salt from the baggies.

Step 9: Ask the child what **color salt** they are using to see if they can **identify the colors.**

Step 10: When the child is done, ask the child to tell you a story about they drew on the paper.

Step 11: Write down the story. Make sure to ask "Who, What, Where, When and Why" questions, prompting your child to continue creating their story.

Step 12: Ask your child what each object is, labeling each object they drew with a yellow highlighter.

Step 13: Ask your child to trace each word in yellow highlighter and to write their name at the top of their story.

Step 14: Ask your child to come up with a Title for their story. The adult should write the title at the top.

B.2 Learning Objectives

Math/Science	Language/Literacy	Problem Solving	Motor Skills
•Use words to describe different textures.	•Write their own name, without help. •Follow three-step directions. •Use sentences in conversation to describe, explain or predict outcomes of real or imaginary events. •Initiate and engage in literacy activities. •Write familiar words by looking at the word then copying.	•Demonstrate Curiosity and ask Questions •Use language to reiterate process and conclusions •Use language to describe objects by a variety of attributes •Identify colors.	•Fine Motor: Use a pen or marker to write familiar words. •Fine Motor: Use a pencil to trace new words

Notes: What did your child do well? Are there any skills they need to continue to work on?

B.3. Shell Homes Activity time: 25 minutes

Materials Needed

☐ One (1) Sea Shell of any size
☐ One (4) Pieces of Paper
☐ One (1) set of Markers/Crayons
☐ One (1) Yellow Highlighter
☐ One (1) Black Pen
☐ One (1) Piece of Blank Paper
☐ One (1) Computer or other electronic device that has access to the Internet

Instructions:

Step 1: Have the child pick up the seashell and place it onto the piece of paper

Step 2: Tell the child to trace the seashell with a marker or crayon.

Step 3: Ask the child about animals that live in shells. There are snails and turtles, but have they ever seen a hermit crab?

Step 4: Watch a video of hermit crabs. The following YouTube video is a wonderful option (1 minute 6 seconds). Seashells Taking A Walk by WildfilmsIndia
https://www.youtube.com/watch?v=uNkq8kKpriM

Step 5: Ask the child to draw a hermit crab on the paper, using the seashell print as its shell.

Step 6: Ask the child to tell the adult a story about the hermit crab in the picture. The adult should use a **yellow highlighter** to write down what they say.

Step 7: Have the child trace the **yellow words** with a pencil.

Step 8: The adult should write the letters of the child's name on a blank piece of paper.

Step 9: Ask the child to come up with a name for the Hermit Crab.

Step 10: The adult should write "Hermit Crab (name of the Hermit Crab that the child created)" on a new sheet of paper:

Example:
Hermit Crab name
Hermit Crab Jessica

Step 11: Ask the child to look at the piece of paper with their name on it, and the piece of paper with the hermit crab's name on it.

Step 12: Ask your child to circle the letters that are the same in their name and the Hermit Crab's name.

Step 13: Ask the child to identify the letters that are different – not in both of the names (what letters that are not circled).

Step 14: Ask the child to write their first, middle and last name on a new piece of paper.

Step 15: Repeat Steps 9 through 11, comparing their full name to the Hermit Crab's name.

Step 16: Ask the child to come up with three new names for the Hermit Crab.

Step 17: Repeat Step 9 through 11 with the three new Hermit Crab names.

B.3 Learning Objectives

Math/Science	Language/Literacy	Problem Solving	Motor Skills
•N/A	•Write their own name, without help. •Use sentences in conversation to describe, explain or predict outcomes of real or imaginary events. •Initiate and engage in literacy activities. •Write familiar words by looking at the word then copying. •Identify all letters by sight and sound	•Use language to describe objects by a variety of attributes •Demonstrate understanding of differences between people, animals, plants and other parts of the planet.	•Fine Motor: Use a pen or marker to write familiar words. •Fine Motor: Use a pencil to trace new words

Notes: What did your child do well? Are there any skills they need to continue to work on?

B.4. Five Oceans Activity time: 30 minutes

Materials Needed
- ☐ One (1) empty water bottle
- ☐ One-quarter (¼) cup vegetable oil
- ☐ One-quarter (¼) cup water
- ☐ Three (3) Cups of Sand
- ☐ One (1) Tablespoon Blue glitter
- ☐ One (1) drop of blue food coloring
- ☐ Access to a map of the world, or access to the Internet.

Instructions:

Step 1: Have the child pour ¼ cup of water into a water bottle.

Step 2: Allow the child to add one drop of blue food coloring into the water bottle.

Step 3: Have the child add two tablespoons of sand to the water bottle.

Step 4: Have the child add ¼ cup of vegetable oil to the bottle.

Step 5: Add one or two pinches of blue glitter to the water bottle.

Step 6: The adult should place the lid on the bottle and close it tightly. Have the child shake the bottle and watch how the waves and sand stay separated. This bottle represents the ocean.

Step 7: Look at a map of the world or view one online (such as this one):
http://www.worldatlas.com/aatlas/infopage/oceansl.htm

Step 8: Now sing the following song while pointing out the oceans on the map. Encourage the child to shake the water bottle while singing the song:

Five Oceans Song by Jeana Kinne
(Sung to the tune "*Frère Jacques*,"
"Five Oceans,
Five Oceans,
On the Earth,
On the Earth.
P is for **P**acific,
A is for **A**tlantic,
And **A**rctic,
And **A**rctic.

I is for **I**ndian,
S is for **S**outhern,
Five, five, five,
Five, five, five,
Five Oceans are on the Earth.
1, 2, 3, 4, 5.
Five Oceans,
Five Oceans."

B.4 Learning Objectives

Math/Science	Language/Literacy	Problem Solving	Motor Skills
•Count using one to one correspondence.	•Use sentences in conversation to describe, explain or predict outcomes of real or imaginary events. •Use songs to learn new information	•Demonstrate Curiosity and ask Questions •Use words to discuss predictions •Use language to reiterate process and conclusions •Demonstrate understanding of differences between people, animals, plants and other parts of the planet.	•Fine Motor: Place small objects into a small container. •Fine Motor: Eye-Hand Coordination

Notes: What did your child do well? Are there any skills they need to continue to work on?

B.5 Sandy Name Activity time: 20 minutes

Materials Needed
- ☐ One-quarter (¼) cup of sand
- ☐ One (1) bottle of Elmer's Glue
- ☐ One (1) Empty paper cup
- ☐ One (1) Small water-color sized Paint Brush
- ☐ One (1) piece of Paper
- ☐ One (1) Marker

Instructions:

Step 1: The adult should write the child's name in large letters (using capital and lower case letters) on a blank piece of paper.

Step 2: The adult should fill one paper cup with 1/8 cup of Elmer's glue.

Step 3: Allow the child to dip the paintbrush into the glue then trace the letters with the paintbrush.

Step 4: Have the child sprinkle sand on the glue using either a plastic spoon or their fingers.

Step 5: Allow the sand set for five minutes.

Step 6: When dry, shake the loose sand off the paper and into a sand bucket.

Step 7: Ask the child to point and name each letter.

Step 8: Repeat Step 2 through 6 using the child's **middle name** and **last name**.

B.5 Learning Objectives

Math/Science	Language/Literacy	Problem Solving	Motor Skills
•Touch new textures (Sand)	•Write their own name, without help. •Introduction to Lowercase and Uppercase Letters •Wriing their whole name (First, Middle and Last)	•N/A	•Fine Motor: Tracing letters.

Notes: What did your child do well? Are there any skills they need to continue to work on?

Gross Motor – Using our large muscles to move!

By Completing Level 3 Activities, We will learn…

- o **Participate in a variety of gross motor activities that require balance and coordination.**
- o **Hop on one foot five or more times.**

Fine Motor – Using our hands to complete tasks

By Completing Level 3 Activities, We will learn…

- o **Use scissors to cut out an object.**
- o **Use a pen or marker to write familiar words.**
- o **Use a pencil to trace new words.**

C.1. Sensory Beach Walk Activity time: 15 minutes

Materials Needed
- ☐ Three (3) empty plastic bins, the size of a shoebox
- ☐ Two (2) cans of spinach
- ☐ Three (3) cups of sand
- ☐ Three (3) cups of water
- ☐ One (1) bath towel

Instructions:

Step 1: Place three plastic bins in a horizontal line **with their sides touching**. Put a towel down at the end of the line.

Step 2: Fill the first bin with sand, the second with canned spinach and the last bin with water.

Step 3: Show the child the bins and tell them that **water** Is In one, **sand** Is in the next one and **seaweed** is in the last bucket.

Step 4: With no shoes on, have the child step into each of the bins.

Step 5: When they step into each bin, ask them what it feels like? Is it slippery, cold, hot, scratchy, etc.

Step 6: When the child is done walking through the bins, have them dry their feet on the towel.

Step 7: Repeat walking through as much as they want!

Step 8: Tell the child that all of these items are in the **Sea.** There are a lot of **Sea Animals** also in the **Sea.**

Step 9: Using sidewalk chalk, the adult should write the word "**SEA**" on the pavement.

Step 10: Ask the child to copy the **"SEA"** with their own piece of sidewalk chalk. If they are unsure how to spell it, have them trace the one the adult wrote first.

Step 11: Tell the child to name some animal names start with the word **"SEA"**. These animals include:

- **Sea** Star
- **Sea** Snail
- **Sea** Urchin
- **Sea** Horse
- **Sea** Lion
- **Sea** Otter

Step 12: Ask the child if there are any other animals they can think of that start with **SEA?**

Step 13: Ask the child to tell the adult a story about the **SEA** and some **SEA** animals that live in it.

C.1 Learning Objectives

Math/Science	Language/Literacy	Problem Solving	Motor Skills
•N/A	•Follow three-step directions. •Use sentences in conversation to describe, explain or predict outcomes of real or imaginary events. •Write familiar words by looking at the word then copying.	•Use language to describe objects by a variety of attributes •Demonstrate understanding of differences between people, animals, plants and other parts of the planet.	•Gross Motor: balance and coordination. •Fine Motor: Trace new words

Notes: What did your child do well? Are there any skills they need to continue to work on?

C.2 Sounds of the Sea Activity time: 15 minutes

Instructions:

Step 1: Ask the child to name some animals that live in the ocean. Do they know what sounds they make?

Step 2: The adult should look for videos or music bits that have the sounds of different sea animals. Play the music or videos and allow the child to listen to the sounds. Can the child identify the animals by the sound they make?

An example of an Ocean Video is: Relaxing Ocean Sounds by Jose Youkis
https://www.youtube.com/watch?v=eGaDOQnUpOI

Step 3: Play the Ocean soundtrack again while the child to uses crayons to draw a picture of the ocean.

Step 4: When the child is done, ask them what is in the ocean they drew.

Step 5: Label each animal that your child draws, using a yellow highlighter.

Step 6: Ask your child to trace each word using a pen.

C.2 Learning Objectives

Math/Science	Language/Literacy	Problem Solving	Motor Skills
•N/A	•Create their own story using imagination and creativity.	•Use a variety of techniques to record information and data collection •Use language to describe objects by a variety of attributes •Demonstrate understanding of differences between people, animals, plants and other parts of the planet.	•Fine Motor: Use a pen or marker to write familiar words. •Fine Motor: Use a pencil to trace new words

Notes: What did your child do well? Are there any skills they need to continue to work on?

C.3 Snorkeling Activity time: 20 minutes

<table>
<tr><td>

Materials Needed

☐ Ten (10) Pipe Cleaners
☐ One (1) Bendy Straw
☐ Access to the internet

</td></tr>
</table>

Instructions:

Step 1: Tell your child that humans can swim in the ocean and see the SEA animals. To do this they need air to breath. One way that Humans can breath under water is to use an air tube and goggles called Snorkeling gear.

Step 2: Watch a video of snorkelers in the ocean. An example is the YouTube video:

Swim with Sharks & Rays Snorkeling Tour from St Regis Resort Bora Bora Honeymoon - Olympus TG-2 by Billy Vollman

https://www.youtube.com/watch?v=dWeS71IIpvY

Step 3: Give the child six or seven pipe cleaners and help them create "snorkeling" gear/goggles out of them.

- Make two circles for the eyes attached together.
- Then attach them to the child's head by attaching two pipe cleaners on each side of the "goggles" by bending the ends of the pipe cleaners around each of the child's ears.

Step 4: Once the goggles are on the child's head, have the child place a Bendy Straw in their mouth, with the end of the straw pointing up.

Step 5: Tell the child they can practice swimming around the room, breathing in and out through the straw.

Step 6: Ask the child to describe what animals they see as they pretend to swim around. When they spot an animal ask the following questions:

- What color are they?
- How many feet do they have?
- What do they eat?
- Where do they live?
- What letter does their name start with?
- What shape are they?

C.3 Learning Objectives

Math/Science	Language/Literacy	Problem Solving	Motor Skills
•N/A	•Use sentences in conversation to describe, explain or predict outcomes of real or imaginary events.	•Demonstrate Curiosity and ask Questions •Engage in problem solving techniques. •Use language to describe objects by a variety of attributes •Demonstrate understanding of differences between people, animals, plants and other parts of the planet.	•Gross Motor: balance and coordination.

Notes: What did your child do well? Are there any skills they need to continue to work on?

C.4. How Big am I? Activity time: 30 minutes

Materials Needed
- ☐ Sidewalk
- ☐ Measuring Tape
- ☐ Sidewalk Chalk

Instructions:

Step 1: Tell the child that an animal called the **Mane Jellyfish** is the **longest animal in the ocean** (120 feet). The **Blue Whale** is the **second longest** animal in the ocean (108 feet).

Step 2: How tall is the child? Measure their height with a measuring tape and tell them how many feet tall they are.

Step 3: On the ground outside, measure out 120 inches (to represent the jelly fish, which is really 120 feet). Draw a line **120 inches long** with sidewalk chalk.

Step 4: Next to the line in Step 3, measure out 108 inches (to represent the blue whale – which is really 108 feet). Draw a line **108 inches long** with sidewalk chalk.

Step 5: Next to the line in Step 4, measure out the length of the child (in inches) and draw a line that length (in inches) with sidewalk chalk.

Step 6: Ask the child: "Which line is longer?"

Step 7: Ask the child to walk each line, placing one foot in front of the other.

Step 8: Ask them to stand at one end of the line and count the steps it takes for them to walk to the other end of the line.

Step 9: The adult should use sidewalk chalk to write the total number of steps it takes the child to walk each line.

Step 10: Ask the child to look at all the number and identify which number is **more.**

Step 11: Ask the child to look at all the number and identify which number is **less.**

Step 12: Ask the child which line is the **longest.**

Step 13: Ask the child to identify which line is the **shortest.**

C.4 Learning Objectives

Math/Science	Language/Literacy	Problem Solving	Motor Skills
•Count up to 20 objects, using one to one correspondence. •Recognizes the names of Numerals. •Understands size words (Smaller vs. Larger). •Show understanding of measurement by using measuring tools.	•Follow three-step directions. •Use sentences in conversation to describe, explain or predict outcomes of real or imaginary events.	•Use words to discuss predictions •Use language to reiterate process and conclusions •Use a variety of techniques to record information and data collection •Demonstrate understanding of differences between people, animals, plants and other parts of the planet.	•Gross Motor: balance and coordination.

Notes: What did your child do well? Are there any skills they need to continue to work on?

C.5 The Dolphin Dance Activity time: 15 minutes

Materials Needed

☐ Access to the internet
☐ Seven (7) pieces of blue colored construction paper
☐ Seven (7) pieces of green colored construction paper
☐ Seven (7) pieces of red colored construction paper
☐ Tape

Instructions:

Step 1: The adult should cut the blue pieces of construction paper into **7 triangles**.

Step 2: The adult should write the number one through seven on each blue triangle, writing one number on each triangle.

Step 3: The adult should cut the green pieces of construction paper into **7 circles**.

Step 4: The adult should write the number one through seven on each green circle, writing one number on each circle.

Step 5: The adult should cut the red pieces of construction paper into **7 squares.**

Step 6: The adult should write the number one through seven on each red square, writing one number on each square.

Step 7: Tape shapes in the form of a large circle, on the floor.

Step 8: Watch a video of dolphins **jumping** in and out of the Ocean.

The following video on YouTube, is a great example: Two Dolphins Jump Out of the Ocean - Stock Footage by Wazee Digital: **https://www.youtube.com/watch?v=g8RoFdyYY3s**

Step 9: Ask the child how **dolphins dance**? That's right… **they jump!**

Step 10: Turn on music of your choice. Have the child **jump around the circle** of **shapes** on the floor. Make sure they're landing on one shape when they're jumping.

Step 11: After 15 seconds, pause the music. When the music pauses, have the **child freeze, stopping on one shape**.

Step 12: Ask them to identify the **color** of construction paper they are standing on.

Step 13: Start the music again.

Step 14: Stop the music and ask the child what **shape** they are standing on. What makes it that shape (How many sides does it have)?

Step 15: Stop the music and ask the child what **number** they are standing on.

Step 16: Start the music.

Step 17: Stop the music and ask the child to identify **all 3 characteristics of the paper they are standing on:**
- What shape is the paper
- What is the color is the paper
- What is the number is on the paper?

Step 18: Repeat Steps 10 through Step 17 at least seven more times.

Step 19: Did you know that dolphins have fins, not legs? It is hard to jump with no legs. Let's try hopping on one foot instead!

Step 20: Repeat Step 10 – 17 while **hopping on one foot**!

C.5 Learning Objectives

Math/Science	Language/Literacy	Problem Solving	Motor Skills
•Recognizes the names of Numerals. •Describe shapes by at least two characteristics. •Identfy Colors.	•Follow three-step directions.	•Demonstrate Curiosity and ask Questions •Use language to describe objects by a variety of attributes •Demonstrate understanding of differences between people, animals, plants and other parts of the planet.	•Gross Motor: balance and coordination. •Gross Motor: Hop on one foot five or more times.

Notes: What did your child do well? Are there any skills they need to continue to work on?

Themed Project – Photosynthesis

Purpose: To teach the process of finding answers to new questions. Each project guides adults and children through investigating specific questions about the theme. The project starts with the development of a hypothesis that is then tested and researched, concluding with an answer to the hypothesis. Specific Learning Objectives include:

Problem Solving Skills: By Completing Level 3, We will learn…

- Predict the results of a familiar action.
- Develop strategies to solve a problem.
- Communicate memories about a sequence of related events that happened in the past.
- Put materials or objects together in new and inventive ways.
- Participate in challenging multi-step activities/projects
- Demonstrate Curiosity and ask Questions.
- Use words to discuss predictions.
- Use language to reiterate process and conclusions.
- Use a variety of techniques to record information and data collection.

Includes: Activities and discussions that address all areas of academic and developmental skills that meets the Level 3 Learning Objectives. Includes math, science, literacy, art, health/safety, gross motor skills, fine motor skills, music and movement and literacy development.

Order of Operation: These projects are designed to be followed in the order they are laid out, each activity building on the knowledge acquired from previous activities.

Project Objective:

When this project is completed, your child should be able to answer the following question:

How do animals breathe under water?

Introduction - What lives in the Ocean?

Step 1: Ask the child to draw a picture of the ocean and what animals live in the ocean.

Step 2: When they are done drawing their picture, ask them what they drew and ask them how do they think that the animals live underwater.

Step 3: Write down exactly what they say on a separate piece of paper.

Step 4: Ask the child: "How humans are able to see the animals that are in the ocean?"

Step 5: Tell them there are a lot of different ways to see the animal life. There are people that Snorkel, Scuba Dive, Fish, Whale Watch and others who drive machines under the ocean (like Submarines).

Step 6: Watch a video of someone scuba diving. A wonderful example is the You Tube video:

Bali Diving HD by Bubble Vision: https://www.youtube.com/watch?v=2uUk9K9TQhg

Step 7: Ask the child what the scuba divers were doing under the water? How were they able to stay under water for so long?

Step 8: Keep the piece of paper from step 3 to revisit when the project is completed.

Investigation

✏ **Activity #1 – Oxygen**

Materials Needed
- One (1) empty two-liter bottle
- One (1) straw
- One (1) roll of tape

Instructions:

Step 1: Explain that humans have to bring oxygen with them under water in order to breathe. The large tanks that scuba divers carry on their backs (shown in the previous video) were full of oxygen.

Step 2: Let's practice breathing like a scuba diver under water.

Step 3: Tell the child to place the straw in the opening of the two-liter bottle, holding one end of it.

Step 4: Using tape (any kind), secure the straw to the two-liter bottle, with one half of the straw sticking out of the bottle.

Step 5: Let's practice breathing like a Scuba Diver!

- Tell the child to breathe in through their mouth, **breathing in the oxygen from the bottle**, and breathing **out through their nose**.

- Have them take up to **three breaths**, then take a break from breathing through the straw.

- How does that feel? That is how you would breath from an oxygen tank underwater.

- Tell them that everyone who goes under the water needs to bring their oxygen with them.

✒ Activity #2: Ocean Divisions

Materials Needed
- Five (5) Pieces of Blue Construction Paper
- One (1) Piece of Brown Construction Paper
- Six (6) White Index Cards (3"x5")
- One (1) Box of Markers
- One (1) Roll of Scotch Tape
- One (1) Blank Wall or Hard Floor (Indoors or outdoors)

Instructions:

Step 1: There are many different layers to the ocean. Ask the children if they know what animals live at the top of the ocean and what animals live at the bottom.

Step 2: Tell the child that animals live all throughout the ocean. There are many animals that live at the **bottom of the ocean** that humans can't see because these animals live at **32,000 feet below the top of the water.** That is very far down!!

Step 3: The adult should write down the following words on the white index Cards. There should be one word per index card:

1) Land

2) Epipelagic Zone

3) Mesopelagic Zone

4) Bathypelagic Zone

5) Abyssopelagic Zone

6) Hadalpelagic Zone

Step 2: Place the five pieces of blue construction paper in a vertical line.

Step 3: Now place the piece of brown construction paper to left of the top piece of blue construction paper.

Step 4: Tape the index card that says, **"Land"** onto the brown piece of paper.

Step 5: Tape the rest of the index cards onto the blue paper in the following order:

1. The **"Epipelagic Zone"** on the top piece of blue construction paper, the level of water right at the surface of the ocean.

2. The **"Mesopelagic Zone"** is underneath the "Epipelagic Zone".

3. The **"Bathypelagic Zone"** is underneath the "Mesopelagic Zone".

4. The **"Abyssopelagic Zone"** is underneath the "Bathypelagic Zone".

5. The **"Hadalpelagic Zone"** is the area of the ocean on the very bottom of the ocean.

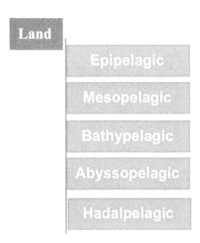

Step 6: The following is a list of animals that live in each of the zones. Tell the child to pick **one or two animals for each zone and draw** them on the blue construction paper with the corresponding index card.

1) **Epipelagic Zone** – Seaweed, Dolphin, Blue Whales, Jellyfish, Sharks, Sea Turtles

2) **Mesopelagic Zone** – Squid, Crab, Swordfish, Krill

3) **Bathypelagic Zone** – Sea Stars, Octopus, Large Whale

4) **Abyssopelagic Zone** – Deep-Sea Anglerfish, Giant Squid

5) **Hadalpelagic Zone** – Sea cucumbers, Jellyfish, Decapods